"Bishop Ellis's willingness to address the process we must go through in order to obtain the promises of God is absolutely phenomenal. This book will give readers the push, language, & strategies necessary to progress forward and remain faithful until what they are believing for has fully manifested. I highly recommend this extraordinary piece of literature for anyone who feels as though they are stuck in the wilderness of life.

This book is written with a clarity and simplicity that any person can understand. Bishop Ellis will give you revelation that will guide you into your manifestation. After reading this, you will be empowered to handle your 'in between'!"

–Pastor Jonathan "YPJ" Miller
Sr. Pastor, Faith Apostolic Miniseries (F.A.M)

God has a great plan and destiny for your life yet navigating the ups-and-downs can be challenging! Bishop Neil C. Ellis has the solution. In his new book, The In-Between, he will guide you through how to handle life's most difficult moments with grace. This book is a must read for anyone on a pursuit for their destiny and in need of encouragement along the way!

–DeVon Franklin, Producer & Best-Selling Author

Bishop Ellis provides a truly amazing road map to fulfilling one's assignment despite the turbulence and upheaval from life's toughest moments. The turning of each page brings about new insight, encouragement and Kingdom Principles to not just survive but thrive. Because of the comprehensive approach to victorious living, this book poses to be a dynamic training manual for both church groups and corporations alike. It is a trailblazing, must read. There is one precautionary note. Upon concluding this book one may find that issues which pledged them for seasons may dissipate giving way to a new found freedom and grace.

–Bishop Joel R. Peebles, DD,DHL
Sr. Pastor, City of Praise
Upper Marlboro, Maryland

"Bishop Neil C. Ellis' sage wisdom and spiritual guidance has guided the who's who of clergy, celebrities, politicians, business people and dignitaries across the globe. Now, everyone gets to experience the wise counsel of this respected man as he helps us navigate the path to our purpose in his latest book, 'The In-Between: The Journey Between Your Dream and Destiny.' This insightful roadmap to achieving your best life will show you why Bishop Ellis has earned the distinction of being your favorite leader's favorite leader!"

–Jawn Murray, TV Host & Pop Culture Expert

In-Between is a literary masterpiece. It is an enlightening and compassionate narrative that forces readers to examine their personal relationship with God and reflect on what it truly means to achieve one's dreams and destiny. Congratulations to a magnificent man of God and a dynamic author.

–Attorney Willie E. Gary

"Bishop Neil C Ellis in this book makes it perfectly clear that we have the talent, skills, and ability bestowed within us by God. It is imperative that we use our faith, trust, and love of God to complete the journey to our destiny knowing that God never gives us more challenges than we can handle. We must trust our God within us to complete our journey to our destiny."

–Thomas W. Dortch, Jr., Chairman Emeritus of
100 Black Men of America, Inc. and President and
Chief Executive Officer of TWD, Inc

I've always found it peculiar that God is identified as Alpha and Omega meaning the beginning and the end but is never recognized for being in the middle. It's striking that when Jesus was crucified however he was placed in the middle. So many of us die in the middle. My bishop, Neil C. Ellis has penned a prescription for people who are in between so that you breathe in the go between. Reading this book will invigorate you to push to the end.

–Dr Jamal H Bryant, Pastor, Author, Philanthropist

The most populated location for most people is a place called 'In-Between'. It's a place where you are neither 'here nor there', 'up nor down', 'above nor beneath'. This book is more than just a great read. It is a revelatory resource that serves as a road map showing us the way to 'next'. It teaches us how to 'de-mystify' our 'not-there-yet' seasons. And, to see God's hand guiding us to our prophesied place. This book is the fresh intelligence from God that we have been desperately seeking. Read it and share it because in it you will discover the footprints that will lead you 'out of' your stagnation and 'into' perpetual movement in God.

–Dr. Carolyn Showell, Ph.D
Dean, The Senior Shepherds Academy

Understanding the purpose for which one is created, and the assignment given is an essential component for successfully embracing the totality of the human experience in a way that pleases our Heavenly Father. Equally imperative is the requisite knowledge needed to effectively navigate life en route to the actualization of said assignment. In ***"The In-Between"***, Bishop Neil Ellis takes you on an exegetical excavation that serves as a manual of instruction and directional compass through the nuances of life lived *between* understanding the purpose of the assignment for your life and the actual procurement, manifestation, and realization of that purpose.

–Dr. Craig L. Oliver, Sr.
Pastor, Elizabeth Baptist Church
Atlanta, Georgia

In-Between

The journey between your dream and destiny

Neil C. Ellis

WORD & SPIRIT
PUBLISHING

In-Between
ISBN: 978-1-949106-13-8

Published by Word and Spirit Publishing
P.O. Box 701403
Tulsa, Oklahoma 74170
wordandspiritpublishing.com

CONTENTS

Foreword ix

Introduction xv

Chapter 1 **Your Destiny Is Your Dream**....................1

Chapter 2 **God's Dream**...9

Chapter 3 **It Starts with a Dream**..........................17

Chapter 4 **Relationships**...25

Chapter 5 **The Opposite of Your Dream**................37

Chapter 6 **God Is with Us**.......................................47

Chapter 7 **Watch Your Attitude**..............................61

Chapter 8 **Obstacles of Your In-Between**...............71

Chapter 9 **Prosper Where You Are**..........................97

Chapter 10 **Serving Your Way into Fulfillment**........109

Chapter 11 **It's Time to Dream Again**....................127

Chapter 12 **Created to Solve a Problem**.................137

Foreword

Every now and then the Lord blesses His Body and the world with a unique gift that challenges, confronts and changes those who experience that gift. When God speaks through and uses Bishop Neil C. Ellis and the anointing that rests on his life, those who experience that release, are often saying what Dr. John Gunn says, **"Now, what am going to do with this?"** It often appears that Ellis uses a different Bible version from the rest of us. He has a rare ability to talk to the text. He seems to ask the text questions that most of us don't ask and see things that most of us don't see. Dr. Darius Daniels says those who walk closely under the hand of God are given **"eyes of an eagle."** Eagles have vision that puts it in a category distinctly different from other birds. It can see for miles. It can see movement under objects. It can detect objects that other birds fly over. **Such is the hermeneutical eye of Bishop Neil C. Ellis.**

Ps 86:12

I will praise you, O Lord my God,
with all my heart;
I will glorify your name forever. NIV

The psalmist makes a declaration. For the remainder of his life, he will praise and glorify the Lord. Praise and worship is both a popular part of contemporary Christendom and a significant segment of the worship experience of many churches today. **We are a praising people.** We praise Him in the song, we praise Him in the dance, we praise with the fruit of our lips with affirmations and declarations of our love for the Lord and our commitment to His kingdom. The **146th, the 147th, the 148th, the 149th** and the final exhortation of the last psalm, the **150th**, command the people of God, "praise ye the Lord" and closes the hymnbook of Israel with **"let everything that hath breath, praise the Lord."** We are a praising people.

But the psalmist does not stop with praise. The writer proclaims his intention to **"glorify the Lord for ever more."** I suspect that the action and process of glorifying God, albeit also part of our sanctified vernacular, just might be a more nebulous term. What does it mean to glorify the Lord? How do we glorify God? We say it. We sing it. But how do you do it? For further insight into this query let's journey into the last gathering of our Lord with His disciples. Let's listen in on the Lord's prayer. I know many of us refer to Jesus' prayer in the Sermon on the Mount as The Lord's Prayer. However, careful analysis of this prayer reveals that this is not the Lord's Prayer, but more accurately, should be labeled The Disciples' Prayer. Jesus could never have prayed the so-called Lord's Prayer due to the line He instructs us to pray daily, **"forgive us..."** Jesus, the spotless, sinless Lamb of God, had no sins for which to be forgiven! Jesus prays "the Lord's Prayer" in John 17.

Now zoom in the lens of your attention in on how Jesus begins His prayer. "Father, the hour has come. Glorify Your Son, that Your Son also may glorify You...I have glorified You on the earth. I have finished the work which You have given Me to do." There it is. Jesus says, "I have glorified You" So whatever it means to glorify God, Jesus did it. In fact, not only do we learn that Jesus glorified the Father; He tells us how He did it. In His prayer in John 17:4, Jesus says " I have brought you glory on earth by completing the work you gave me to do". NIV "I glorified You on the earth, having accomplished the work which You have given Me to do. NASU. I think the late Eugene Peterson says it best in his uninspired The Message paraphrase: Jesus said,

"I glorified you on earth by completing down to the last detail what you assigned me to do."(from THE

MESSAGE: The Bible in Contemporary Language © 2002 by Eugene H. Peterson. All rights reserved.)

Jesus tells us, He glorified the Father by **doing, finishing, completing down to the last detail what the Father "assigned" Him to do.** There it is. According to Jesus, we glorify God when we do our assignment! In **"The In-Between"**, Neil Ellis takes you on a journey filled with **exhortations, instructions,** and **revelations** on the **value,** the **mandate** and **significance** of doing your assignment. You have one. God gave it to you. This work addresses the dynamics of living your destiny and completing your assignment. With **wisdom, insight** and **divine revelation,** Bishop Ellis calls us to walk in the destiny and assignment that God ordained from the foundation of the world.

While a student at the University of Illinois, I took a class in Criminology. To this day, I have no idea why I took this class. In fact, I cut the class every way but loose! It was one of those classes where your class grade was based on one assignment. We have a paper due that would determine your academic outcome. As I said, I cut the class often. In fact, I only learned by accident that this paper would due within a few weeks. I immediately went to work trying to get the paper out. I scanned the reading list, I spent time in the library, I burned the midnight oil, and consumed much No-Doze. By the time the paper was due, I miraculously turned it in on time. In fact, I can remember both proudly and arrogantly lightly slamming my paper down on the professor's desk. The following week, papers were returned, with what would be the grade for the semester.

Now you know you're in trouble when the professor writes notes on your cover page! The notes said, **"Good paper. Good content. Good research."** I beamed with pride at first glance until I kept reading to the last note at the bottom of the page. The notes in the middle said, "Good paper. Good content. Good research" and at the bottom in bold letters **"THIS WAS NOT THE ASSIGNMENT!" GRADE "F"** and the failing grade was written in red ink, with a circle around it. I thought it was a bit crass and carnal for the man to put the F in red ink and put a circle around it. An F is just as much an F in black ink! But he clearly said, with no chance of misinterpretation: "This was NOT the assignment." O that we may never stand before and hear him say, **"Good career. Great buildings. Good congregation. Good reputation." But "This was NOT your assignment."**

I can testify of the tragedy we face is doing the wrong assignment. However, even when you identify your assignment, another mountainous challenge arises.

Bishop Neil Ellis declares **"assignments often come with limited information."** Ellis meticulously weaves the principle of divine assignment into the fabric of dreams producing a tapestry of destiny while highlighting the indefiniteness of the phase he calls **"in-between."** It's the in-the-mean-time in-between time that so often discourages and defeats us.

Welcome to an exciting excursion into the mind and will of God concerning your life. May the Spirit of the Living God, open your eyes, your mind and your spirit to hear what God will say through the mouth and words of this gifted prophet. You have a destiny. You have an assignment that takes you into that destiny. May you be blessed in your processional through the **in-between seasons** of your journey. May you glorify God by walking in destiny. You glorify God the way Jesus did; by doing your assignment even in **the in-between times.**

Kenneth C. Ulmer, DMin, PhD
The King's University

Introduction

Have you ever dreamed of arriving at a place in your life where you will flourish and function on a level where you can do everything that you believe you were created to do? In the words of John Sculley, "The future belongs to those who see possibilities before they become obvious."

All persons, regardless of their spiritual persuasions or religious convictions, have at least one thing in common: our destiny and reason for living are wrapped up tightly in our dreams that will take us from point A to point B. It is true, God has plans for our life. Listen to Jeremiah in the eleventh verse of the twenty ninth chapter of the book that bears his name:

"For I know the plans that I have for you, saith the LORD, plans of peace, and not of evil, to give you a future and a hope." In that same regard, we all have something else in common: the need to survive everything that we are confronted with in-between point A and point B.

So often, my friends, believing God is not the problem for the people of God. Trusting God enough to step out in faith is usually not the issue. Believing God to do what He said He will do and receiving all that God has placed in our Spirit is not usually the challenge for so many of us. Getting up from where we are and taking the journey that leads us to our destiny, for most of us, is a no-brainer. The real challenge for most of us is surviving all of the obstacles and difficulties we may face **in-between** where we are and where we are going.

Your God-given assignment is so important to God that He gave you that assignment, long before your conception.

From what we know of God, one of the things that is very important to Him is *assignment*.

Your God-given assignment is so important to God that He gave you that assignment, long before your conception.

Before God formed you, before He squeezed you into shape and tucked you into your mother's womb, God

KNEW you, CHOSE you, and GAVE you your LIFE assignment...all before you were conceived.

> Then the word of the Lord came unto me, saying, Before I formed thee in the belly I knew thee.
>
> —Jeremiah 1:4–5

So, God gave you an assignment, brought you from the heavenly realm to the earth realm, and then put everything in place for the effective fulfillment of that assignment. GOD has invested heavily in YOU, and GOD will fight to protect HIS INVESTMENT.

One of God's most remarkable claims is found in the book of Isaiah. It speaks to His knowing the ending from the beginning. God ends things, and then He begins them. In the Spiritual realm, He fixes the ending and then He begins it in the physical realm and releases us on our journey toward our destiny. The challenge is that He never tells us of the **in-between** stuff, the things we will be confronted with along the way.

So often our present set of circumstances do not look anything like what God said to us about our destiny or where He said He would be taking us. Many times, just as soon as God has painted a picture and given us a glimpse of where we are headed, we immediately experience the complete opposite.

It should be noted that the journey is just as important as the destiny itself.

Why is all of this necessary?

It is necessary because there are lessons to be learned along the way. These lessons include:

- Lessons about God
- Lessons about how we ought to relate to Him
- Lessons about how we draw on His power
- Lessons about how we stay connected to Him
- Lessons about overcoming trials with His help

This is why embracing destiny is not enough. We must also embrace the path God has put in place for us to get to our destiny.

As we make the journey toward our destiny, we should not fight the process; instead we should follow the path. It should be noted that the journey is just as important as the destiny itself.

The process may at times be painful, but pain processes the assignment and prepares you for the platform. Once you hit the platform, then pain is what empowers you for the performance. The process may at times be painful, but in the end, it will be profitable.

As you read the principles laid out in this latest of my literary works, I believe it will help you to handle all of the **in-between** stuff that you will encounter on your way to your destiny.

Enjoy the journey!

In-Between

The journey between your dream and destiny

CHAPTER 1

Your Destiny Is Your Dream

There is a place in which you will thrive, and a position in which you will flourish. There is a grand purpose for you to fulfill, and people in this world whom only you are uniquely equipped to help in the way that they can receive it. There is a way of life reserved especially for you. It is a life full of abundance and hope, a life full of love and family. What I'm describing is not a fantasy or some kind of wishful thinking. It is the reality of the true Christian condition that can only be produced by living a life of faith. This lifestyle is not thrust upon us as Christians, though; it's something we must contend for and fight to protect. God has given to each of us an assignment. Along with that assignment, He gave us the tools and the passion to accomplish it. The Bible says:

> *So, we are convinced that every detail of our lives is continually woven together to fit into God's perfect plan of bringing good into our lives, for we are his lovers* ***who have been called to fulfill his designed purpose.*** *For he knew all about us before we were born and* ***he destined us from the beginning*** *to share the likeness of his Son. This means the Son is the oldest among a vast family of brothers and sisters who will become just like him.* ***Having determined our destiny ahead of time, he called us to himself and transferred his perfect righteousness to everyone he called.*** *And those who possess his perfect righteousness he co-glorified with his Son!*
>
> —Romans 8:28–30 TPT

Assignments often come with limited information. There is a phrase in Genesis 12:1 that we often overlook, yet it's very significant when it comes to understanding the assignments of God. As God called Abram to leave his country and his family, God told Abram to go... "unto a land that I will show you." Simply put, God made it very clear to Abram that He was not going to release all the details to him at once, but that He would give details on a "need to know basis."

Why did the Lord choose not to give Abram all the details at once? After all, God is all-powerful and He can do whatever is pleasing to Himself. Could He not have told Abram what the future held? Absolutely! Yet God was interested in Abram staying close to Him in an intimate relationship. Had God given Abram a complete roadmap to the mountain, Abram might have started off, but not have remained close to the Lord...depending upon Him, listening to Him, and allowing Him to be in complete control.

When God gives to you an assignment, He may not release all the information to you at that time, but He always has the end in mind. It's in the in-between that we need to survive with little or no information.

Limited information is not a sign that God doesn't know what the future holds. Since God is almighty and all-knowing, He knows exactly what is coming in each day. Yet, when God withholds information from us, it is a call to us to stay close to Him, to depend on Him, to lean on Him moment by moment, day by day. In truth, God has very significant reasons for withholding information

from us. He knows quite well the independent nature of mankind, and so He does what is necessary to cause us to depend upon Him. In truth, mankind functions best with "limited information." Although Abram didn't know where the place was that he was to go, God made it His business to release to Abram all the information that he needed when it was vital and significant. When God gives to you an assignment, He may not release all the information to you at that time, but He always has the end in mind. It's in the in-between that we need to survive with little or no information.

Your assignment is so important to God that He gave it to you long before your conception. Then He put you in right standing with Him. He made sure your dream was bigger than you, so that you would need Him in order to fulfill it. God has plans for you, not only to accomplish great things, but also to be great! God isn't about transforming your situation; God is about transforming you and letting you transform your situation. He wants your life to emulate your older brother, Jesus, and to have an intimate relationship with God that exudes faith and love. He wants dynamic power to be made available in your life, through yielding to the Holy Spirit, and through contending for God's greatest and best. And the best part about all of this is that there is nothing you can do to earn the call, and nothing you have done, or could ever do, that will cause you to lose your call, along with the gifts and talents He gave specifically to you to accomplish that call. He said as much in the book of Romans:

> *And when God chooses someone and graciously imparts gifts to him, they are never rescinded.*
>
> —Romans 11:29 TPT

This assignment, along with all of the things God has placed inside of you, and the plans that God has put in place for the fulfilling of your assignment, constitute what is called **destiny.** It is God's design, purpose, and predetermined path for your life.

There is another word used to encompass all that a destiny is: **DREAM.**

Although it may not be apparent to everyone that they have a destiny, even though they do, it is irrefutable that everyone has a dream. Christian or non-Christian, rich or poor, sick or healthy, whatever your condition or position, everyone has a dream. To say that God has a destiny for your life can sound cold, and distant, or seem as if God is just giving you a set of orders to follow. But, to say that God has a dream for you, that takes on a new meaning. That means you haven't been alone in dreaming about a better way to live; that God has been dreaming of a day when you as His child would be happy, at peace, and close to Himself. He hasn't been looking down at you with disdain, or with disappointment, but with longing. He is longing for you to accept His gifts, to accept His help, to take charge of your life and audaciously press on to fulfill your purpose. He placed His desire, His passion for people, in you. That desire manifests uniquely in each one of His children. It manifests as their own personal dream, a desire and passion to fulfill a God-designed purpose in the earth, a creative vision for the future, deep inside, that speaks to your soul. It draws out in us the best parts of ourselves, drawing on the limits of your gifts, talents, and abilities. It brings clarity to your highest ideals and sparks a sense of purpose in your day-to-day life. It produces in you a fiery passion to please God with the fulfillment of all that He has placed inside you.

Now, you may be thinking that this all sounds great, but that you don't know what you're supposed to do. You might not know what God wants to do in you and through you. You don't have any grand dreams, just a desire not to live from paycheck to paycheck. Well, I have good news for you: you are in good company. As God told Abraham:

> *"Get out of your country, from your family, and from your father's house, to a land that I will show you."*
>
> —Genesis 12:1 NKJV

God basically told Abraham that He was calling him to a purpose that He would tell him about later. So, if you heard that you're called, and you have no idea what that calling entails, then congrats. You are perhaps just like the greatest man of faith, besides Jesus, who has ever walked the face of the earth. And if you are discovering your dream, or if you come across something you're passionate about and wonder if it is from God, then keep this in mind:

The only way to know what your dream is, or to know whether your current dream is from God, is to actually know God.

Patrice and I have been married for almost 40 years (1983); I know her voice anywhere; in the dark, in the light, or in a crowd. I know her voice anywhere, especially if she is calling my name. No one calls my name the way that she does, because every time she calls me by my name, there is something that happens inside of me. I recognize the voice of the person who has been with me through thick and thin all these years. I know her voice anywhere, but that's after many years; that's relationship, that's communication. We communicate often, we talk, we get along, we agree, we disagree, but we are husband and wife and I know her. I know her voice anywhere. That's how you get to know when God really speaks to you. You have to build a relationship with

Him, talk to Him often, and let Him talk back to you. God hardly ever says anything new to us. Most of the time He is just telling us what He has already said to us in His Word,the Bible. He always confirms what He tells us through the Bible and He never contradicts the Bible. So, while you're getting to know God, I can tell you the perfect place to start on your path toward your destiny. I can tell you God's perfect plan and purpose for your life for today, and even this very moment. It's to love your neighbor as yourself, and to love God with all your heart, soul, mind, and strength.

By doing that, you'll find yourself on the same journey that birthed this book; the journey from where you are, to where you are going.

CHAPTER 2

We Are God's Dream

The first step in learning how to navigate your *in-between,* is understanding where God comes in on your journey toward your dream. The best place to start is where God did in Genesis, where we learn the first thing we know about God: that He is the Creator.

He spoke everything that is good, all that we see and know, into existence. Though I would argue that the planet may have come into being when God spoke it, it was birthed as part of His dream long before that. We forget sometimes why God made the world in the first place. After existing for an eternity, a desire and a dream grew in His heart, one that many of us can relate to: a dream to have children.

> *God spoke:* ***"Let us make human beings in our image, make them reflecting our nature so they can be responsible for the fish in the sea, the birds in the***

air, the cattle, and, yes, Earth itself, and every animal that moves on the face of Earth." God created human beings; he created them godlike, reflecting God's nature. He created them male and female.

—*GENESIS 1:26–27 MSG*

We have a God-given destiny, a place of fulfillment and purpose for us to accomplish and enjoy.

God had a dream, a passion, and a desire to have lots of children. From that dream, an immeasurable amount of power was released to bring that dream to fruition. He created the universe because He needed a place to put the galaxy. He made the galaxy because He needed a place to put a solar system. He created our solar system because He needed a place to put our planet. He created the world because He needed a place to put His children. All of the grandeur of the universe was created as the result of a dream. It places value on us that we should meditate on more often; it gives meaning to why He would go to the length of sending Jesus to die a brutal death in order to buy us back. You see, before we go any further and discuss how to bring about the manifestation of the dream God has placed inside of us, we must first understand this simple truth: ***We are God's dream.***

We have a God-given destiny, a place of fulfillment and purpose for us to accomplish and enjoy. In order to accomplish our destiny, there is a journey we are all required to take. God never intended for this journey to ever be taken alone. God wants to take this journey with us. He wants to **strengthen us, help us, undergird us, guide us, fill us with peace and joy, teach us, comfort us, and be with us.** This is why it's not enough to just be obedient to what God said; we have to be willing to be obedient. He wants us to have a good attitude as we enjoy the journey growing our faith, and ultimately growing our relationship with Him. In short, the true power behind our destiny, behind the dream that God put inside of us in the first place, can be summarized in this statement:

My dream is not about me; it is about us.

It's not about what I can accomplish; it's about what God and I can accomplish together. Life becomes a glorious adventure with a relationship that transcends this life into the next one; the relationship between a Father and His dear child.

There is such a powerful verse that puts this into perspective for us:

> *Yes, furthermore, I count everything as loss compared to the possession of the priceless privilege (the overwhelming preciousness, the surpassing worth, and supreme advantage) of knowing Christ Jesus my Lord and of progressively becoming more deeply and intimately acquainted with Him of perceiving and recognizing and understanding Him more fully and clearly. For His sake I have lost everything and consider it all to be mere rubbish (refuse, dregs), in order that I may win (gain) Christ (the Anointed One).*
>
> —PHILIPPIANS 3:8 AMP

Many people have lived their lives in the **in-between** phase, and they never get to the promised land because they miss this truth. They live for the promises instead of living for the One who made the promises to them. The truth is that **the journey toward the fulfillment of your destiny is just as important as your destiny itself.**

This revelation is threaded all throughout the Bible, if you are looking for it:

> *Even though I walk through the sunless valley of the shadow of death,* ***I fear no evil, for You are***

> ***with me;*** *Your rod to protect and Your staff to guide, they comfort and console me.*
>
> —PSALM 23:4 AMP, emphasis mine

> *And what agreement has the temple of God with idols? For you are the temple of the living God. As God has said:* ***"I will dwell in them and walk among them. I will be their God, and they shall be my people."***
>
> —2 CORINTHIANS 6:16 (NKJV), emphasis mine

> ***My dear children, you come from God and belong to God.*** You have already won a big victory over those false teachers, ***for the Spirit in you is far stronger than anything in the world***
>
> —1 JOHN 4:4 (MSG), emphasis mine

This isn't even scratching the surface of how often God calls our attention to the fact that we are His children, and that He is with us. Adam and Eve only got to talk to God in the cool of the morning, and while God was away, they succumbed to the temptation of the serpent and fell into sin. So, this time around, after God bought us back, He didn't send an angel with His guidance and power. No, He sent His very own Spirit to reside in us, so we have the assurance that we are never alone to fend off the temptation ourselves.

For no temptation (no trial regarded as enticing to sin), no matter how it comes or where it leads has overtaken you and laid hold on you that is not common to man that is, no temptation or trial has come to you that is beyond human resistance and that is not adjusted and adapted and belonging to human experience, and such as man can bear. But God is faithful to His Word and to His compassionate nature, and He can be trusted not to let you be tempted and tried and assayed beyond your ability and strength of resistance and power to endure, ***but with the temptation He will always also provide the way out (the means of escape to a landing place), that you may be capable and strong and powerful to bear up under it patiently.***

—1 Corinthians 10:13 AMP, emphasis mine

God has strategically placed that dream inside of you and that you two can and will accomplish it together.

So, while we are journeying toward our dream, and while we are experiencing what seems to be insurmountable odds, we know that God is with us and He will make sure that whatever test, trial, or challenge we come up against can be defeated by faith. Even if the sheer gap between where you are and where God has called you to causes you to be dismayed, don't fret. Have confidence that God has strategically placed that dream inside of you and that you two can and will accomplish it together.

CHAPTER 3

It Starts with a Dream

Dreams are not merely the nightly thoughts you experience as your brain sorts out the day's events. They are the goals and visions that ignite the fire within your heart and saturate your soul with joy at the very thought of them. They are those continuing visions of what you want your life to be at its highest level of fulfillment; what you want to do; how you want to do it; and what kind of person you want to become in the process.

Your destiny and reason for living are wrapped up tightly in your dreams and desires, like the genetic information inside a seed. That dream in your heart contains the very blueprint for who you are.

Your dream is that idea, that vision for your life that burns inside of you...something you can't ignore for long. It keeps coming back to your mind because it is part of who you are; it will never leave you alone.

A dream doesn't drive you; it draws you. It is like a huge magnet that pulls you toward it.

Your dream did not originate with you. It resides within you, but it's from God. God put it there. He is the source of your dream.

There are many examples in the Scriptures of patriarchs whose lives portrayed principles that can help us to understand how to handle the confusing **in-betweens.** David, who was anointed to be king of Israel, was told that he was going to lead the nation of God's chosen people. He was chosen and anointed to be king, and then he was sent back out to watch the sheep! Several years would pass before he would become king. He was anointed to be king at the age of fifteen, but he did not occupy the throne until he was thirty. There were fifteen years of **in-betweens in his life.**

Jesus Himself was anointed to be the Savior of the world. He was born the King of all creation, yet His ministry didn't start until He was thirty years old! He tried to jump-start His ministry when He was twelve years old, when His parents found Him in the temple teaching the "rulers." His mother quickly shut Him down, and we do not hear of Jesus again until He was thirty years old. There were eighteen years of **in-between in His life.**

The Bible is **chockfull** of powerful destinies that were only accomplished after a great journey was completed. (Again, the journey is just as important as the destiny itself.) One story especially stands out when it comes to navigating and handling the confusing **in-betweens**; it is the story of Joseph. I will use his story as the backbone for this book to guide us through the **in-betweens**. For those of you who don't know the story of Joseph, or who want a quick reminder, I'll give you a quick recap of his life.

God gave Joseph a literal dream in which his father and brothers were bowing down to him. After Joseph shared this dream with his brothers and father, his brothers, (who already disliked Joseph because they felt that their father favored him most) decided that they had had enough of Joseph. At first planning to murder Joseph, they opted to sell him into slavery instead. Joseph was then bought by Potiphar, an Egyptian captain. As a slave, Joseph, through his faithfulness and the favor of God, rose to the position of head of Potiphar's household. After all that Joseph had experienced up to this point, he was then falsely accused of a crime by Potiphar's wife, which ultimately led to him being thrown into prison. Eventually, as a prisoner,

Joseph rose to the position of head of the prisoners and interpreted two inmates' dreams while he was there. A couple of years passed, and then the Pharaoh had a dream he needed to have interpreted after none of his own magicians were able to interpret the Pharaoh's dream. Joseph interpreted the Pharaoh's dream, and Pharaoh placed Joseph in a position of prominence and authority. It was a position that Joseph was then able to leverage in order to save his entire family.

Our successes of tomorrow depend largely on the dreams we are having today. Never be afraid to dream!

There are so many powerful messages throughout the story and life of Joseph about how a young man went from a slave to becoming the second-in-command of one of the largest nations in the world at that time.

And remember, it all started with a dream!

Genesis 37:5 (NKJV) begins, ***"Now Joseph had a dream."***

We should never underestimate the power of a dream, because each of us has the strength to make our dreams come alive. Our successes of tomorrow depend largely on the dreams we are having today. Never be afraid to dream!

The Bible says:

> ***Do not despise these small beginnings, for the Lord rejoices to see the work begin,*** *to see the plumb line in Zerubbabel's hand.*
>
> —Zechariah 4:10 NLT

God likes to see His children dreaming. It's the beginning, a preview of what He has planned for our lives. You can know it is a dream from God when it consumes you, and it usually requires your talents, skills, gifts, and abilities. Although the dream is the beginning of the journey, it will remain dormant until you do one simple thing: **tell it!**

The more you tell your dream, the more you become your dream. You will never see the fulfillment of your dream until you become your dream; you have to live it. **And if you want to live it, you have to tell it.**

- A dream is your creative vision for your life in the future. Tell it!
- A dream is a vision deep inside that speaks to your very soul. Tell it!

- A dream speaks to your highest ideals and sparks in you a sense of destiny. Tell it! Nothing is as real as a dream.

Your visions and your dreams are the children of your soul, the blueprints of your desires.

The world can change around you, but your dream will not.

Because the dream is within you, no one can take it from you.

In my view, the single most important difference between successful people and non-successful people would have to be their the ability to dream, their ability to see things the way they should be or could be.

When you see it, tell it!

Anything you want to become, do, or have during your lifetime, can be considered your dream.

Your visions and your dreams are the children of your soul, the blueprints of your desires.

The more your dream is talked about, the more you are able to imagine it and the more you're able to see yourself accomplishing it. It is faith! Faith comes by hearing and hearing the Word of God. The more you talk about your God-given dream, the more faith develops in your heart to pursue that dream. It stirs up your passion and ignites the creative side of your brain with all the ideas of how you and God can accomplish your dream together.

Oftentimes in the ***"in-betweens,"*** your life does not mirror your dreams. Sometimes it looks completely opposite to the dream God gave you. Joseph had a dream. For much of his journey to the palace, his circumstances did not match his dream. It is important at this point to keep talking about your dream when, like Joseph, your life doesn't reflect anything that even remotely resembles your dream. **Talk about it** until it resonates with your spirit. The more you talk about it, the more resolute you become in pushing for the reality and pursuing the fulfillment of it. When your dreams are told to the right people, they'll be able to rejoice with you and help you accomplish it.

Yet, **there** are many people who never talk about their dreams because of the fear of what people might say. Because of fear, some people hold back their dreams, keep them to themselves, and never give their dreams life. You should not allow fear to prevent you from talking about your dreams with anyone. Rather you should be cautious when deciding who you share your dreams with. They must believe in you if they are to believe in your dreams. Joseph learned this lesson the hard way. Joseph told his brothers his dreams, but instead of supporting him, they vehemently opposed him and determined that the only options they had of getting rid of him and his dreams, were that of human trafficking and murder! So often the people you look to for encouragement, support, and strength at strategic times in your life, **go against you or do not support you.** This can be disheartening, and even frightening. There are people who will try to steal it or kill it, even though a God-given dream can never die. Seek God's direction in regard to who you should share your dreams with.

CHAPTER 4

Relationships and Your Dream

Throughout the Scriptures, it is clear that God is an advocate of relationships. Most of the great men and women of the Bible had a strong supporter, someone whom they were in close relations with. Whenever God gives you a dream, He usually gives you someone to support you and to ensure that your dream becomes a reality. For example, Elisha had Elijah; Joshua had Caleb; and David had Jonathan. If you are convinced that your dream is from God, expect to cross paths with this person who has been anointed to stand by you. Know this: The one person whom God will give you will provide enough strength in your life to make up for the hundreds or thousands of people who don't support you. Oftentimes this very special individual will be your spouse. This person is called, anointed, and equipped to stand beside you. It's rare that God would call you to a vision and not also sensitize your spouse to that vision. So, cherish your spouse because without them, you will never be able to achieve your dream. They are your first actual ministry. The Bible says:

> *As the church is subject to Christ, so let wives also be subject in everything to their husbands. Husbands, love your wives, as Christ loved the church and gave Himself up for her.*
>
> —EPHESIANS 5:24–25 AMP

Your relationship with your spouse is the most important relationship you will ever have outside of your relationship with God. You must see that and place a premium on your relationship with your spouse if you hope to accomplish your dream. Your spouse is used by God to strengthen you in ways that a thousand other people singing your praises never could. Your spouse has seen you at your best and at your worst, and yet they will have such a love for you and believe in you all the same. Your spouse makes up for all of the negative feedback you will ever hear from the world while you are on your path to achieving your dream.

- **Creation was a reflection of relationship: "Let US"**
- **The Trinity exists in relationship: Father, Son and Holy Spirit.**

- **Eve was created for Adam for relationship.**
- **God came down in the cool of the day to be with Adam as a demonstration of relationship.**
- **The first thing Satan attacked was the relationship between God and man and then later the relationship within the family, Cain and Abel.**

It is important for you to be aware that there will be people who will not believe in or understand your dream. You may be discouraged or distracted by their negative responses. However, don't give in! Remember, it is the enemy's job to do all in his power to destroy the dreams that God has given you. Do not allow the enemy to use those who oppose you to cause you to lose focus of your dream.

When it comes to Joseph's life, he certainly had difficulty with his brothers, and it is likely that most would assume that the father's reaction was similar to that of the brothers', except it was less murderous. I don't believe this is the case based on what we know about Joseph's father leading up to this point. I'm convinced that there was a far deeper meaning within the interesting exchange between Joseph and his father when Joseph was telling him his dream. In Genesis 37:11, it appears that Joseph's father was not in support of his dream. The Scriptures say that his father rebuked him.

The word ***rebuke*** that was used in the text is a formal expression of disapproval. However, the ***Message*** translation uses the word ***brooded*** instead of ***rebuke.*** This word means to be engaged in showing deep thought about something that makes one sad, angry, or **worried.** Joseph's father seemed to have grasped the weight of what his son's dreams meant. The Scriptures say that he "kept the matter in mind." This is similar to what the mother of Jesus did at His birth: "She pondered these things in her heart." At the time of Jesus' crucifixion, she was able to draw on them when everybody else walked away from the cross.

It seems that Joseph's father saw Joseph's dreams as more than just dreams. He asked his son a question for clarification: "***Does this means that one day your mother and I and your brothers will bow down before you? Is that what you're saying, Joseph?***" And when his father raised the question for clarity and interpretation, his brothers envied him even more. They were not pleased that their father seemed to be supporting Joseph. Their negative feelings continued to escalate. They hated him, then they envied him, and finally, they envied him to a greater degree.

Similarly, we can expect those around us to respond much the same way.

It's interesting to note that in spite of the deep hatred and the tremendous lack of support from those whom he looked to for support, Joseph kept dreaming.

When you start dreaming, there will be people in your life who may not be pleased with your dreams. There may be some people in your life who will hate you because you continue to dream. Do not allow people's responses to cause you to let go of your dreams or stop you from dreaming again. One of the things I like about God is that when He gives you a dream, He will not allow you to let it go.

You have the right to dream, and everybody else has the right to decide whether they believe in you or not, but they don't have the power to stop you from dreaming. I'm aware that if God gives me a dream and I'm satisfied that it is from God, even if others don't support it, that means I'm not going to put my dreams on hold. No, I'm going to keep dreaming and working on their fulfillment until I make that person a believer. The best way to make a detractor shut up is to make sure your dream is fulfilled. Fulfill the dream! People reserve the right to choose whether or not to support you. You should not dismiss people because they are not as excited about your dream as you are. And you should not get angry with people because they choose not to help you fund your dream. It's your dream!

For the most part, people will flow with you—until you start dreaming.

Others will only flow with you until you start talking about your dream.

Then there are those who will go with you only until you start pursuing your dream.

Joseph's brothers envied him. Look at this carefully: The envy came from the house. You know what I'm beginning to realize: The people who work with you, the people who hang with you, and the people who are related to you are always alright with you as long as you remain "under" them; but if you ever start to elevate yourself, then their attention and support take on new meaning. The minute God helps you and you begin to make progress in your life, many of the people around you will feel like it's their job to knock you down a peg or two and bring you back to reality.

For the most part, people will flow with you until you start dreaming.

Others will only flow with you until you start talking about your dream. Then there are those who will go with you only until you start pursuing your dream. Once you start going after your dreams, EXPECT some relationships to change...and SOME relationships will not survive to see fulfillment, because dreams have a way of separating you from people...especially non-dreamers. Dreamers are risk-takers and are always in the minority. Dreams will separate the **risk-takers**, from **caretakers and undertakers.**

It's interesting to note how it appears to be such a major task to celebrate one another's future. It takes a lot of love and humility for a boss, parent, peer, or family member to celebrate your success instead of envying it. Our families have seen us when we were at our worst, and sometimes it is hard for them to see us in any other light. So, don't let it surprise you that when God gives you a dream, the people He uses to support you in the beginning are those people to whom you are not really connected. Often it just takes time for the people who have grown up with you and seen you when you made poor choices, to finally accept the change that God has worked in you and through you. In some cases, it never happens, but that shouldn't stop us from praying for them and accomplishing our dreams anyway.

So, whether they are for you or against you, it is important that you are able to identify people and things that are sent to prevent you from fulfilling your dream. Even Jesus faced opposition on the way to the cross. The Pharisees were constantly looking for ways to trap Jesus. The enemy's intention was to use them to destroy God's plan for humanity. He even tried to use one of Jesus' most trusted friends, Peter. In Mark 8:33, Peter loved Jesus so much that he did not want Jesus to be harmed in any way. Unfortunately, he did not see the entire plan. Beware: Sometimes opposition can unintentionally come from those whom we love. This is why you must be vigilant, focused, and intentional when it comes to the fulfillment of your dream. Knowing who your supporters are as well as your opposition is paramount to successfully handling your **in-between** and ultimately fulfilling your dream.

Once you know the persons who are on your team, your supporters, and the persons who are on the opposing team, those who oppose your dream, then you can start the game, and begin your journey to see the fulfillment of your dream. It's time to play to win! So, stay focused and keep moving.

You must be intentional, adamant, and willing to fight for your dream. Joseph did not allow the negative responses of his brothers to deter him. He kept on dreaming. He kept on telling his dream. Like Joseph, we, too, must not let the negativity of others stop us from dreaming and seeking to fulfill our dreams.

It is also apparent from scripture that because Joseph kept dreaming, his second dream had more details than the first one. God made the message clearer, which provided him with a sharper perspective. **This could never come from friends. This comes from the decision to keep dreaming.** This is what really brings your dream into perspective. When you keep your hands in God's hands and stay connected, you will not stop dreaming and nothing will be impossible.

Thomas Hawkslee states:

> *"I am unaware of anything that has the right to be called impossibility."*

The world as we know it has been shaped by dreams. All of the great achievements in our universe were once considered to be impossible.

A man with a dream is a lot more powerful than a man with the facts.

Facts once said that electric lights were impossible, but Thomas Edison's dreams made them a reality.

Facts once said that man would never fly but the Wright Brothers' dreams changed all of that.

It does not matter what your dream is; if you are satisfied that it is a God-given dream, it is possible.

It does not matter what your dream is; if you are satisfied that it is a God-given dream, it is possible. Not everybody has to see it, believe it, or believe in you, but the dream is possible. We know how important relationships are. We know how much help they can provide, and your dream could never get done without others joining in to help outside the miraculous. This is because God wants us to work together. That being said, you don't have to wait around for someone to come support you. Just go out and be someone worth supporting. Faith is an act! So act like your dream is a reality regardless of what anyone else thinks or says. Know that you already have the most stacked team regardless of who else joins you. You have God, Jesus, and the Holy Spirit. I think Romans 8:31 (amp) says it best:

What then shall we say to all this? If God is for us, who can be against us? Who can be our foe, if God is on our side?

CHAPTER 5

The Opposite of Your Dream

It is imperative that you understand that not only people can oppose you or become an opposition. Sometimes your present set of circumstances can be so diametrically opposed to your dream that you can allow them to actually become an opposition to your dream. You must then be prepared to face the opposite of the dream while you are on your way to accomplishing your dream.

> *Then his brothers went to feed their father's flock in Shechem. And Israel said to Joseph, "Are not your brothers feeding the flock in Shechem? Come, I will send you to them." So he said to him, "Here I am."*
>
> —GENESIS 37:12–13

Joseph experienced this many times on his journey to the palace. In the dream that Joseph had, he saw his brothers bowing down to him but his present reality in the text had him serving his brothers. What Joseph was currently doing was not what he saw himself doing in the dream. That is what causes many people to become confused and discouraged; they want to live today on what they dreamed yesterday. It is an attitude of instantaneous gratification. **Whatever happened to learning how to lean, depend on and wait for God?** So many of us want instantaneous gratification, and that's why a lot of people, because of this spirit, are missing out on their dreams. If it isn't fulfilled in a week, they turn away from it. Whatever happened to patience? Whatever happened to endurance? Whatever happened to hard work? Why do we so quickly turn away from the in-between stuff? Why don't we take a page out of this psalm written by David: "*My soul wait silently for God alone, for my expectation is from Him*" (Psalm 62:5 nkjv).

So, Joseph, in the dream, saw his brothers bowing. Don't forget now, his father interpreted this dream, so he saw the brothers bowing too; but now his father sent Joseph out **to serve those whom he saw in the dream serving him.** What a good father!

Like Joseph, David was anointed to be king, but his ***in-between*** did not look anything like what a person anointed to be king should look like. His life was diametrically opposed to that of a king's life. He went back to taking care of his sheep, serving his brothers, and eventually serving King Saul. During this period, he had to run for his life on many occasions. Your dream may cause you to experience the opposite of all that you hope to accomplish. Knowing the inevitability, we need to gird ourselves up, and as I said before, prepare to face it!

In Genesis 37, the brothers mocked Joseph as if it was a sin to dream: "*Now when they saw him afar off, even before he came near them, they conspired against him to kill him. Then they said to one another, "Look, this dreamer is coming!"*"

Take careful note, my friend. If you don't deal with that **hatred** in your heart, you will be promoted to the class of **envy,** and if you do not arrest and deal with envy, you are going to be elevated to the category of **a murderer**. You have to learn how to catch these things and nip them in the bud. If you realize that there are some crazy things going on in your mind and in your spirit, and that you're having funny thoughts about certain people, you have to know how to go to God and say: "If You find anything in me that does not represent You, please take it away." If you don't, that thing is going to fester. There are so many people today **who** cannot fulfill their dreams, **all** because they have too much envy in their heart for other people who are dreaming.

The Word admonishes us in Psalm 51:10 (KJV):

Create in me a clean heart, O God; and renew a right spirit within me.

Unfortunately, Joseph's brothers left their hatred unchecked, and as a result, they became obsessed with killing their very own brother, and destroying his dream. His physical death was not their aim; it was the by-product of their hatred of Joseph and their disdain for Joseph's dream! In verse 20, it says:

"Come therefore, let us now kill him and cast him into some pit; and we shall say, 'Some wild beast has devoured him.' ***We shall see what will become of his dreams!"***

Okay, please don't miss this. The possibility for the fulfillment of a dream will always threaten some people. You will never escape all the dream killers. Sometimes, in order to kill your dream, they have to try to kill you—not necessarily kill you in the flesh, but they will go after your character, your reputation, and your integrity. They will try to kill your courage, and they will try to kill your spirit.

But don't be afraid for one second; try as they may to kill us, we are protected. Hear this comforting word from God Himself:

> *But no weapon that is formed against you shall prosper, and every tongue that shall rise against you in judgment you shall show to be in the wrong. This peace, righteousness, security, triumph over opposition is the heritage of the servants of the Lord, those in whom the ideal Servant of the Lord is reproduced; this is the righteousness or the vindication which they obtain from Me this is that which I impart to them as their justification, says the Lord.*
>
> —ISAIAH 54:17 AMP

This verse should rise up in your spirit any time you begin to feel opposition! God will not call His children to a divine purpose, which will attract the attention of the kingdom of darkness, and then leave us to fend for ourselves. He filled His Word with promises to protect us:

> *But the Lord is faithful, who will establish you and guard you from the evil one.*
>
> —2 THESSALONIANS 3:3 NKJV

> *Be strong and of good courage, do not fear nor be afraid of them; for the Lord your God, He is the*

One who goes with you. He will not leave you nor forsake you.

—DEUTERONOMY 31:6 NKJV

It's up to us to meditate on these verses whenever we come under assault, whether it comes from the inside or the outside. Let me illustrate. One day when I was nine years old, my grandfather told me, "Boy, you are going to pastor a great church one of these days." God used him to speak to me. When I was fourteen years old, and a student at St. John's High School in Nassau, The Bahamas, I received a telegram from Bimini advising me to come to Bimini right away. My grandfather, "Papa," was dying, and he had sent for me. I got to Bimini four days later, and about 5:00 p.m. on the day of my arrival, Papa had me kneel by his bedside, and he laid his hands on me. At 3:30 a.m. the following day, he died. As I remember now, on his deathbed Papa said, "Boy, you will pastor a great church one day", but Papa never told me about the rumors, the lies, the rejection, the persecution, and the betrayal that would come my way.

Papa never told me about the tabloid stories. Papa never told me about the backstabbers. In essence, Papa never told me about my **in-betweens.** Papa just said, "Boy, you will pastor a great church one day." You see Papa (Rev. Robert Ellis Sr.) was the pastor of the Mt. Zion Baptist Church in Bimini (one of the family of islands in The Bahamas, and the island of my birth). I went to Papa that day because, at a church meeting the evening before, the members did not treat him too kindly. When I visited Papa the following day, and I asked him, "Why did the church people treat you so badly?" his response was, "Boy, you will pastor a great church one day." He never told me, and I didn't have enough sense right then to understand what he was trying to tell me. The difference in our experiences was that, with Papa it happened from people "in the house." For me it came from people outside of the church.

In thirty-two years, from 1987 to 2019, I've never had any real problems in Mount Tabor. I have never had to address a church issue or crisis. I have never had a challenge with my leadership. I have never had any uprising or any rude behavior or any intolerable actions. All the trouble I've ever experienced came from outside of the church, which was fine. I had made up my mind a long time ago that I was not going to allow anyone or anything to stop me from dreaming or to stop me from believing until the fulfillment of my dreams. Because of what Papa told me, I made up my mind that, as long as what they were saying on the outside didn't affect what was happening on the inside, I would pay little or no attention to it.

God never shows you or explains to you your in-between. He just shows you your destiny, so that you will know when you get there.

So, when you feel your opposition breathing down your neck and you hear them conspiring against you, be encouraged! Satan may try to stir up a mob against you, but all that means is that you are causing some major problems for him! You know that you have a covenant with God, that you are His child, and that you are covered by His protection. So I say, let them talk about you, let them TRY to stop you, let it be in the news, in the papers, let every form of opposition come against you, because YOUR GOD IS BIGGER! You are more than a conqueror! Joseph wasn't deterred when he experienced the opposite of his dream; nothing about a pit was in Joseph's dream. In the dream, the brothers were not evil. They were actually bowing down. In the dreams the brothers were not the ones with the power and authority. It was Joseph. So, what's happening here? "I just had this wonderful dream in which God showed me my future and what it would look like and now I'm dealing with this?"

Let me tell you something: God never shows you or explains to you your **in-between.** He just shows you your destiny, so that you will know when you get there. God will never show you all the stuff you have to go through to get to what He has destined you for. This is what Isaiah 46:10–11 (MSG) has to say:

> *Think about this. Wrap your minds around it. This is serious business, rebels. Take it to heart. Remember your history, your long and rich history. I am God, the only God you've had or ever will have—incomparable, irreplaceable—From the very beginning telling you what the ending will be,* ***All along letting you in on what is going to happen...***

God leads step by step, telling us our destination, but He doesn't tell us our path to get there. If He did, there would be no need for faith. So even when your life does not look like your dream, trust God that it's only a matter of time before it will!

CHAPTER 6

God Is with You

I want to begin this chapter by pointing you to the greatest motivational and inspirational book that has ever been written, The Holy Bible, the word of God. I invite you to pay close attention to the entire thirty ninth chapter of the first book in the Bible, Genesis.

> 1 And Joseph was brought down to Egypt; and Potiphar, an officer of Pharaoh, captain of the guard, an Egyptian, bought him of the hands of the Ishmeelites, which had brought him down thither.
>
> **2 And the LORD was with Joseph,** and he was a prosperous man; and he was in the house of his master the Egyptian.
>
> **3 And his master saw that the LORD *was* with him, and that the LORD made all that he did to prosper in his hand.**

4 And Joseph found grace in his sight, and he served him: and he made him overseer over his house, and all *that* he had he put into his hand.

5 And it came to pass from the time *that* he had made him overseer in his house, and over all that he had, **that the LORD blessed the Egyptian's house for Joseph's sake;** and the blessing of the LORD was upon all that he had in the house, and in the field.

6 And he left all that he had in Joseph's hand; and
he knew not ought he had, save the bread which he
did eat. And Joseph was *a* goodly *person*, and well
favored. 7 And it came to pass after these things,
that his master's wife cast her eyes upon Joseph;
and she said, Lie with me.

8 But he refused, and said unto his master's wife,
Behold, my master wotteth not what *is* with me in
the house, and he hath committed all that he hath
to my hand; **9** *There is* none greater in this house
than I; neither hath he kept back any thing from me
but thee, because thou *art* his wife: how then can I
do this great wickedness, and sin against God?

10 And it came to pass, as she spake to Joseph day by day, that he hearkened not unto her, to lie by her, *or* to be with her.

11 And it came to pass about this time, that *Joseph* went into the house to do his business; and *there was* none of the men of the house there within.

12 And she caught him by his garment, saying, Lie with me: and he left his garment in her hand, and fled, and got him out.

13 And it came to pass, when she saw that he had left his garment in her hand, and was fled forth,

14 That she called unto the men of her house, and spake unto them, saying, See, he hath brought in an Hebrew unto us to mock us; he came in unto me to lie with me, and I cried with a loud voice:

15 And it came to pass, when he heard that I lifted up my voice and cried, that he left his garment with me, and fled, and got him out.

16 And she laid up his garment by her, until his
lord came home. **17** And she spake unto him
according to these words, saying, The Hebrew
servant, which thou hast brought unto us, came in
unto me to mock me:

18 And it came to pass, as I lifted up my voice and cried, that he left his garment with me, and fled out.

19 And it came to pass, when his master heard the words of his wife, which she spake unto him, saying, After this manner did thy servant to me; that his wrath was kindled.

**20 And Joseph's master took him, and put him into
the prison, a place where the king's prisoners *were*
bound: and he was there in the prison.**

21 But the LORD was with Joseph, and shewed
him mercy, and gave him favor in the sight of the
keeper of the prison.

22 And the keeper of the prison committed to
Joseph's hand all the prisoners that *were* in the
prison; and whatsoever they did there, he was the
doer *of it*.

23 The keeper of the prison looked not to any
thing *that was* under his hand; because the LORD
was with him, and *that* which he did, the LORD
made *it* to prosper.

If at this point in your life you are living in obedience to God's word, faith is the holder of your destiny. If you have learnt how to lean and depend on God and trust Him to order and control the affairs of your life, then faith is your servant.

Pay close attention to the highlighted portion above. As you do, know that even now, the Lord is with you. Isn't that comforting to know, especially after recognizing what His continuing presence did for Joseph? God is no respecter of persons. He is the same yesterday, today and forever. Joseph believed that. Do you?

If at this point in your life you are living in obedience to God's word, faith is the holder of your destiny. If you have learnt how to lean and depend on God and trust Him to order and control the affairs of your life, then faith is your servant. There is a place that each of us has been called, chosen and anointed to reach in our lives. It's a place we will never reach by **FOOT**; we will only get there by **FAITH**.

Many people have a false understanding of what faith is. For many, faith is some kind of power or force. They think if they have enough faith, God will do whatever they ask of Him. So when a crisis comes up, they try to move God into action with their faith. When an emergency pops up, they try to use faith like a rope to slip around God's neck and force their will on Him. When disaster comes, they try to use faith like a button they push to nudge God into action. When God does not respond the way they expect Him to, they become disappointed with Him. They feel like God has let them down.

> Faith does not mean that you believe God can do something. He can do it whether you believe it or not. Faith does not mean believing He will do something; that's hope. You hope He will. Faith is believing that He is. Hebrews 11:6

> Now faith is the substance of things hoped for, the evidence of things not seen. Hebrews 11.1

Real faith is **substance** and **evidence.** Substance is spiritual; it's intangible. You can't see it, hold it, taste it or park it; it's intangible. Evidence on the other hand is physical; it's tangible. You can see it, touch it, drive it or live in it. Real faith allows you to hold on to **substance** until **evidence** shows up.

It takes faith to believe in your dream when no one else does. It takes faith to believe that God has your back when you don't see a way out of your situation. It takes faith to cultivate a relationship with your Father God to believe that He is, and to believe that He loves you and is for you. It takes faith to believe that God is with you. It takes faith to please God, and more than that, we are called to live by faith. Faith is predicated on what you do not see. According to Dr. Tony Evans, "Faith is believing that something is so, even when it is not so, that it might be so, simply because God said so."

A heart and mind filled with the word of faith will attack the foundations of all the negative issues in your life. If you are seriously pursuing destiny, life will occasionally hand you something that is difficult to live with. What I'm about to say may shock you: God's favorite part about your dream, in my humble view, is your **in-between.** Now, don't misunderstand me. God doesn't like to see us struggling, in pain, or in lack. He does, however, love to see His children stepping out in faith; He loves to see His children believing more in what He said than in what their problems are saying. This is what the Bible calls "living by faith." Hear how often the Holy Spirit brings this topic up.

> *For therein is the righteousness of God revealed from faith to faith: as it is written, The just shall live by faith.*
>
> —Romans 1:17 KJV

> *Now the just shall live by faith: but if any man draw back, my soul shall have no pleasure in him.*
>
> —Hebrews 10:38 KJV

> *Behold, his soul which is lifted up is not upright in him: but the just shall live by his faith.*
>
> —Habakkuk 2:4 KJV

> *But that no man is justified by the law in the sight of God, it is evident: for, the just shall live by faith.*
>
> —GALATIANS 3:11 KJV

> *For we walk by faith, not by sight*
>
> —2 CORINTHIANS 5:7 KJV

We are supposed to live by faith. We are not supposed to be moved by the **in-between;** we are supposed to be steadfast in our faith. We should be more moved by what God has said than we are moved by what we see. We should be more aware of what God said than what our current situation is telling us. I like how Paul puts it in Philippians:

> *Not that I am implying that I was in any personal want, for I have learned how to be content (satisfied to the point where I am not disturbed or disquieted) in whatever state I am. I know how to be abased and live humbly in straitened circumstances, and I know also how to enjoy plenty and live in abundance. I have learned in any and all circumstances the secret of facing every situation, whether well-fed or going hungry, having a sufficiency and enough to spare or going without and being in want. I have strength for all things in Christ who empowers me. I am ready for anything and equal to anything*

through Him who infuses inner strength into me; I am self-sufficient in Christ's sufficiency.

—PHILIPPIANS 4:11–13 AMP

Paul is saying that the secret to navigating your **in-between** is the same way to navigate the beginning and the end. He's echoing the sentiments that we brought up in the beginning of the book, when we talked about how God wants to be with us every step of the way. It's relying on Christ to overcome; it's living the life of faith. It's operating like Shadrach, Meshach, and Abednego, knowing that there is a fire coming if you stay true to God, but knowing that God will show up right in the middle of the fire with you. It's like Daniel in the lions' den, staying true to God, knowing that, when you follow after Him, He'll shut up the mouths of those trying to devour you. It's like Peter asking God to call him out on the water, knowing that, if Jesus said "Come," then He was offering the power to come.

Ladies and gentlemen, there is no substitute for faith. You have to believe in God, and you have to learn how to be in the fire without feeling the effects of the fire. You have to learn how to rest while surrounded by lions that are seeking to devour you, and how to step out on the water and achieve the impossible because **GOD IS WITH YOU!**

In the story of Joseph,the first time we see God with him, was after he became a slave. This had absolutely nothing to do with the dream:

> *But the Lord was with Joseph, and he though a slave was a successful and prosperous man; and he was in the house of his master the Egyptian.*
>
> —GENESIS 39:2 AMP

You know this is important because it is in direct opposition to how many God-fearing people believe. Many believe that the minute they face any negativity in their lives, it is indicative that God has already left them. I believe this is the general consensus among disappointed and hurting believers. But this couldn't be further from the truth. If that was the case, then just about every person in the Bible, Jesus included, were living out of the will of God for their lives. We need to stop praying that God rescue us from the storm, and we need to start praying for God to give us enough strength to face the storm head-on! Remember what was said in Genesis 39:2: The Lord was with Joseph even though he was a slave. That's right! Joseph was dumped into a pit, sold by his broth- ers, bought by the Ishmaelites, made a slave in Potiphar's house, and yet the Lord was still with him. How else was he able to keep a smile on his face having experienced all of that? That means if you are behind on your mortgage, if you are having a challenge trying to keep food in the house in the midst of your crisis, and you don't know how you are going to pay your bills next week, if you are worried about a business deal, then I have some good news for you: **The Lord is with you.**

"Alright, Bishop, I've been a Christian for fifteen years, so why do I have cancer?"

"I've been serving God all these years, and I've been trying to live the best way I can, but last week the doctor told me I have breast cancer."

I'm so saddened by that, but can I assure you of something? In the midst of the breast cancer, **The Lord is with you!**

"So, my husband and I, we've been serving the Lord and he's been pastoring this church and doing the best that he can with this church. And then the Lord took him home after thirteen years of serving the church, and left me here by myself without my husband."

Unfortunately, life is an interesting mixture of good and bad, but are you open to some great news? **The Lord is with you!**

Get that into your spirit now! In spite of how it looks, **the Lord is with you!** Wherever you are, trust Him and **prosper** right there. **The Lord is with you!**

We are reminded in **2 Corinthians 4:8–9 (NKJV) that:**

> *We are hard-pressed on every side, yet not crushed; we are perplexed, but not in despair; persecuted, but not forsaken; struck down, but not destroyed.*

It doesn't matter how bad it is, somebody is going to be able to see that **the Lord is with you.** Sometimes we need to do what David did and encourage ourselves in the Lord—so say it out loud: **"The Lord is with me."** After all you've been through you can still testify that the Lord is with you. You were down in the dumps, but the Lord kept you; and in the fullness of time, the Lord raised you up. I like how the NIV puts it:

> *And the God of all grace, who called you to his eternal glory in Christ, after you have suffered a little while, will himself restore you and make you strong, firm and steadfast.*
>
> —1 PETER 5:10

Destiny should never be viewed only from the perspective of the good things that happen in your life. Destiny must be viewed from the perspective of the good and the bad, with the knowledge that God has the ability, the power, and the capacity to make them all work together for your good. Don't live your life with the fallacy of assuming that along the road to destiny, you will only encounter good experiences. In contrast, along the journey to your destiny, there will be negative and positive experiences. Who would have thought that in order for Jesus to redeem the whole world, He would have to face the perils of crucifixion? He had to face terrible and degrading things, such as people spitting on Him, people jeering at Him, and being taken from judgment hall to judgment hall. Who would have thought that nails would be put in His hands, a sword through His side, and that He would be forced to die an ignominious death? To fulfill His divine assignment, He needed to endure these things and many more. They were a part of His divine **in-between.** As Christians, we too will face many circumstances that seem unfair, difficult, or nearly impossible to deal with. Like Jesus did, we must endure and successfully handle our **in-between** if we are to see the fulfillment of our God-given dreams. This may seem frightening, and contrary to what is often preached today. Most people avoid any talk of sacrifice and submission, but both are required of us. It's not a popular topic. You see, sacrifice and submission are hard up-front; the thought of them and the anticipation of them are tough for anyone to bear. Jesus Himself asked if there was a way out, if this cup could pass from Him. But Jesus took the brunt of our suffering so that we wouldn't have to. We still have to submit; we still have to sacrifice, and we will still experience pain, but because of what Jesus did for us, we don't have to experience it alone. Like we mentioned earlier, we can be tossed into the fire without feeling the effects of that fire!

So, the question for you is: ***Can you handle the in-between?*** The obvious answer is no.

The real question you should be asking is: Can you handle the **in-between** with God? And the answer to that question is yes! So even when you experience challenges, **I implore you to hold on to Psalm 37:5 (NKJV):**

> *Commit your way to the Lord; trust also in Him, and He shall bring it to pass.*

We cannot change our past.
We cannot change the facts.
We cannot change the inevitable.
However, what we can do, is play
on the one string we have,
and that is our attitude.

CHAPTER 7

Watch Your Attitude

Attitude is more important than facts. It is more important than the past. Attitude is more important than education, money, and circumstances. It is more important than what other people think or say or do. We cannot change our past. We cannot change the facts. We cannot change the inevitable. However, what we can do, is play on the one string we have, and that is our attitude.

God will lead you to the right attitude before He leads you to the right opportunity.

Your expectation will change your **attitude.**

Changing your **attitude** will change your **behavior.**

Changing your **behavior** will change your **performance.**

Changing your **performance** will change your **life.**

A large percentage of the successful fulfillment of your dream is dependent upon your attitude.

Do not allow where you are to make you ***look*** like where you are. This can be a confusing point to be; you don't look like where you've been, and you don't look like where you are now. Learn how to make the best out of where you are. More than likely, where you are now is not what you saw in your dream, but watch your attitude. I like how it's put in the book of Isaiah:

> *If you are willing and obedient, you shall eat the good of the land.*
>
> —ISAIAH 1:19 (NKJV)

It's not enough if you do what God says and grumble and complain about it. You have to do it with good cheer. Even if you are in the midst of a crisis, you should be filling up your time with thanksgiving and praise, not complaining, not calling up all of your friends and talking about how hard your situation is for an hour and then end the conversation with something like, "Well, the Lord will take care of me," and think that makes the past hour of elevating your struggle and complaining okay. You're not thanking God for the trials, but you're thanking God for equipping you to handle them. You're thanking God for His Word, for His Spirit, for sending His Son, and for working in you and through you to accomplish a mighty destiny. You're thanking Him for His companionship, for all the things He's blessed you with. And take note of this: You are thanking Him for what He will do! There is no greater expression of faith than to lift up your hands and thank God for something that you can't see. How are you going to keep a man or woman down when their first response to any bad situation is to give God thanks? There is nothing you can do with a person like that. There is no place for them to go except up! The only reason you would be thanking God when the doctor gives you a bad report is because you've already received a report in which God said that by His stripes you are healed! You can rejoice because you have more faith in that than in what the doctor said. Now, you may feel down. You may feel like complaining, and throwing up your fists, but by faith you thank God for the solution, and then your feelings and thoughts will follow suit. We should be talking about the solution more than we are talking about the problem; we should be thanking God for the realization of our dreams every day instead of rocking back and forth, begging Him for help to make it through the day. We should be happy, and we should be consistent. The world should look at us and think, "What is their secret? They aren't stressed, they aren't tired all the time, and no matter what happens in their lives, they still have a smile, and they are still at peace." Our attitude is our choice, and it should be one of the most powerful witnessing tools we possess.

I like what it says in James:

> *Consider it a sheer gift, friends, when tests and challenges come at you from all sides. You know that under pressure, your faith-life is forced into the open and shows its true colors.*
>
> —JAMES 1:2–3 (MSG)

Consider it a sheer gift, or as one translation says, "count it all joy" when you experience challenges. "Consider it" or "count it"—these are verbs, which mean they are actions that we must take. It's a choice whether you will look at your situation with weariness and doubt, or if you will smile in the midst of the storm because God is with you and there is not an opposition in existence that can stop His destiny for your life. There is another person that comes to mind when I think of maintaining a good attitude, and that is Daniel.

The Scriptures record the events of Daniel's life. As a boy he was trained to honor God through worship and prayer. Then he was captured by the enemy, taken to a foreign country, and exposed to things that went against his training. However, he was determined to hold on to what he believed. He experienced terrible events from the moment he was captured to the time he was honored by the king. According to the Scriptures, though, he maintained an excellent spirit.

> *Then this Daniel was distinguished above the presidents and the satraps because an excellent spirit was in him, and the king thought to set him over the whole realm.*
>
> —DANIEL 6:3 (AMP)

In other words, he maintained a good attitude throughout all of the many terrible things he had to face. This is the standard for fulfilling your dream and reaching your destiny.

Similarly, the events of Joseph's life during his **in-between** were unfair and difficult to deal with. However, he too, chose to approach each circumstance with a good attitude. At various points along his journey, Joseph found himself in some negative situations not by choice. Nevertheless, he made the best out of where he was. At this point in the story, Joseph was a slave in Potiphar's house. He didn't make himself a slave. He was sold into slavery by his brothers. He had every right to be angry in his spirit, but he made the best out of a bad situation. He did not let his slavery affect his positive mentality. He was a slave, but he thought like a king. This is so critical when it comes to your attitude concerning your dream.

All too often we get confused in our **in-betweens;** all too often our identity starts to get wrapped up in where we are instead of where we are going. We often become surrounded by people who have lived their lives in a place that we are just passing through. If we are not careful, we can begin to allow the people around us, our current situation, and the pressures of our **in-between** to conform us into the same mentality of those by whom we are surrounded. You see, there is a difference between a young man of God who works as a slave and a slave. There's a difference between a person who washes dishes and a dishwasher. There is a difference between a shop boy and a boy who works in the shop. Although you may be working at a very humbling job, with very limited pay, surrounded by small-minded people, it's up to you as to whether or not you'll let the mentality, and the character, of your surroundings affect you; if you'll let what's on the outside get on the inside of you. So many people get stuck in their **in-betweens,** as their dreams begin to fade away. They spend too much time focusing on where they were and listening to what other people had to say about them. They should be focusing on what God said His plan was for them. You see, your attitude is so important because you won't progress toward your dream until you get the right attitude. Like I said earlier, God will lead you to the right attitude before He leads you to the right opportunity.

If you're too busy complaining, if you're too busy getting frustrated because your dream hasn't become a reality yet, if you're too busy blaming other people for why you haven't already accomplished your dream, then your biggest enemy to your dream is *you*.

If you don't want to get stuck while pursuing your destiny, hold on to the vision of where you are going. Be the person you see in your dreams! Have the demeanor of somebody who's already accomplished their dream. As you do this, you will become the person who is capable of living out your dream. It starts with you and it starts with your attitude. If you're too busy complaining, if you're too busy getting frustrated because your dream hasn't become a reality yet, if you're too busy blaming other people for why you haven't already accomplished your dream, then your biggest enemy to your dream is *you*. Your attitude is stopping you dead in your tracks on your journey to accomplish your God-given destiny. You've got to determine within yourself which you are, because to the world you're just a shop boy and to the world your dream is just some fantasy, but to the man or woman with a heart full of faith and a mind full of determination, your dream is as real as you are alive, and your future is as real as your present circumstances.

Ability is what you are capable of doing.

Motivation determines what you do.

Attitude determines how well you do it.

I am convinced that life is 10 percent what happens to me and 90 percent how I react to it.

Your attitudes will always become your actions or reactions.

Lou Holtz once put it this way:

"Ability is what you are capable of doing.

Motivation determines what you do.

Attitude determines how well you do it."

The kind of work we do is not as important as the attitude we bring to it. Your living is determined not so much by what life brings you as much as by the attitude you bring to your life.

Experience is not what happens to you; it's what you do with what happens to you. You are responsible. Although you may not be able to prevent the worst from happening, you are responsible for your attitude toward the inevitable misfortunes that darken your life. **The wrong attitude can ultimately cause you to miss a major moment.**

CHAPTER 8

Obstacles of Your In-Between

On the journey to fulfilling your dreams, there are obstacles that can hinder you from reaching your destiny. These obstacles are the same for everyone, and although many of us usually trip over one of them as opposed to all of them, one is all it takes to hinder and sometimes stop us from accomplishing our God-given destiny.

God didn't promise days without pain, laughter without sorrow, or sun without rain, but He did promise strength for the day, comfort for the tears, and light for the way. If God brings you to it, He will bring you through it.

The good news is that although there are various kinds of obstacles, the solution to all of them is the same. The easiest way not to trip over something is to realize where the object is. So, in this case, I'm going to warn you of some of the tricks your enemy has up his sleeve so you can avoid the obstacle whenever it comes up.

The First Obstacle Is Unforgiveness.

Robert Louis Stevenson, in one of his books, tells of **two sisters who never married, living together in the same house,** but who fell out and decided never to speak to each other again. So with **a piece of chalk** they divided up every area of their house. **With a piece of chalk** they drew a line across the sofa. They drew a chalk line right through the middle of the kitchen, and even the doorways were divided. The two women lived the rest of their lives **imprisoned in bitterness.** They refused even to acknowledge each other's presence. **With a piece of chalk, they marked each other completely out of their lives.**

**When and if you fail to forgive,
the person you consider
your enemy will direct your life
via remote control.**

People are still drawing chalk lines. Perhaps we don't see them, but they are there. Something real or imagined happens, and the result is, **"I don't want anything more to do with you. You're not my friend. I'm drawing the chalk lines. This is my side; that is your side."**

May I ask you a question? Do you keep a list of people who've hurt you or mistreated you? Keeping a list of offenders sends a strong message to yourself that:

1. **You have not yet forgiven them.**
2. **You still have a strong desire to get back at them.**
3. **You somehow want to make them experience the pain they caused you.**

Let me remind you of some words from Dick Armey, "You cannot get ahead while you are getting even."

Bitter people think that they are hurting the people they are angry with when in fact they are only hurting themselves. When and if you fail to forgive, the person you consider your enemy will direct your life via remote control.

It matters not who we are, or what our social, political, religious or financial status is in life, if we want to see the finish line and get to the place of destiny, we must develop and maintain the capacity to forgive, let go and move on. **Forgiveness is the only way I know to let go.** Our tomorrow must include a world where forgiveness is practiced and reconciliation is embraced. In order to forgive, you must let go of your resentment, bitterness, hurt and pride. You've got to be willing to let go of your list.

The story of Joseph gives us a model for forgiveness. He was a person, about whom the Old Testament says practically nothing negative. But let's not forget: in his life, there was **Abuse, Affliction, Accusation and Abandonment.** But, God was with him. Joseph learned in long, lonely, and dark days to trust God when he had every right not to.

The past had shattered Joseph's ability to trust his brothers. His brothers hated him, despised him, put him in a pit, and sold him into slavery. The famine that God revealed to Pharaoh in the dreams that Joseph interpreted, had come and was in full effect.

There was no food growing anywhere. The bible describes the famine as **worldwide**. There was **universal suffering everywhere in the known world,** except in one place; Egypt. In Egypt, all the grain stored during the years of plenty by a capable and faithful administrator, was now available and was being distributed. As fate would have it, his brothers were in front of him anxiously awaiting his verdict that would have determined the course of the rest of their lives. He could've bless them or destroy them. But, Joseph didn't harbor any un-forgiveness toward any of them. After he became second-in-command, he didn't line them all up and execute them for committing all of these atrocities against him. Instead he saved the lives of his brothers and father, gave them a better life than they had known, and made Egypt more prosperous than ever; increasing the prosperity of the rest of his offenders.

**If we harbor a grudge,
nurse an offense, and don't forgive,
then resentment builds in
your hearts and you'll remain
a prisoner to our pain.**

If you are going to achieve your dreams, you cannot hold on to the past. You cannot let the offenses of others drag you down to their level. God forgave you; let that same love flow through you and cause you to forgive others. A heart full of the love of God, producing an abundance of forgiveness, can be the most powerful testimony that you can ever give.

Let all bitterness, wrath, anger, clamor, and evil speaking be put away from you, with all malice. And be kind to one another, tenderhearted, forgiving one another, even as God in Christ forgave you.

—Ephesians 4:31–32 (NKJV)

We've all been deeply hurt in some way: betrayal by a spouse, a behind-your-back criticism from a friend, hateful judgment from someone at church, a false accusation by a co-worker, unfair treatment by a boss or a parent. The deeper the hurt, the harder it is and the longer it takes us to forgive. If we harbor a grudge, nurse an offense, and don't forgive, then resentment builds in our hearts and we'll remain a prisoner to our pain.

I like what Nelson Mandela said after being wrongfully imprisoned for twenty-seven years:

> **"As I walked out the door toward the gate that would lead to my freedom, I knew if I didn't leave my bitterness and hatred behind, I'd still be in prison."**

> "To forgive is to set a prisoner free and discover that the prisoner was you."
>
> Lewis B. Smedes

If you permit bitterness and un-forgiveness to grow in your life, it won't be long until they kill your joy, steal

your peace, and destroy your focus and ultimately your future. When you can't focus, you can't win. And when you can't win, it's difficult to watch other people win without becoming bitter about their success. You won't be able to celebrate anybody else's success. Before you know it, you've become a hater.

Joseph had every opportunity, and what many would incorrectly think, every *right*, to harbor unforgiveness toward practically everyone in his life: his brothers for wanting to kill him and then selling him as a slave, his father for being fooled and never coming to save him, Potiphar for throwing him in jail after all Joseph had done for him, Potiphar's wife for lying about him, and even the butler for waiting two years before telling what Joseph had done for him. There is one last element of unforgiveness that can halt your progress toward your dream, and it's when you don't forgive yourself. The only cure for this is found in Christ. I like what Corrie Ten Boom says:

> "There is no pit so deep, that God's love is not deeper still."

> For the Lord of hosts hath purposed, and who shall disannul it? and his hand is stretched out, and who shall turn it back?
>
> —ISAIAH 14:27

God is saying

> "Who can stop My plan?
>
> Who is more powerful than I am?
>
> I created the whole universe.
>
> Who can make a mistake so big that I can't forgive it?
>
> Who can have a problem so large that I can't solve it?
>
> Who can have a dream so great that I can't bring it to pass?"
>
> All of the forces of darkness combined together cannot keep you from your destiny.

I know sometimes we think that because we have made mistakes in life, our actions must have stopped God's plan. But, I say this to you very respectfully:

YOU'RE NOT THAT POWERFUL! None of your mistakes surprise God. He already has the mercy for it in place.

You have to spend time with the Lord and His Word and choose to believe that His love is greater than any sin or mistake you could ever make. The Bible sums it up in this passage from the Message translation:

My dear children, let's not just talk about love; let's practice real love. This is the only way we'll know we're living truly, living in God's reality. It's also the way to shut down debilitating self-criticism, even when there is something to it. For God is greater than our worried hearts and knows more about us than we do ourselves. And friends, once that's taken care of and we're no longer accusing or condemning ourselves, we're bold and free before God! We're able to stretch our hands out and receive what we asked for because we're doing what he said, doing what pleases him. Again, this is God's command: to believe in his personally named Son, Jesus Christ. He told us to love each other, in line with the original command. As we keep his commands, we live deeply and surely in him, and he lives in us. And this is how we experience his deep and abiding presence in us: by the Spirit he gave us.

—1 John 3:18–24

For most of your life you have been fighting with yourself.

For almost all of your life, you've been pulling against yourself.

For most of your life, you've been sabotaging yourself and your assignment.

You could have been where you're going a long time ago.

You have to let go of what could have been, how you should have acted and what you wish you would have said differently. You have to accept that you can't change the past experiences, opinions of others at that moment in time. When you finally recognize that truth then you will understand the true meaning of forgiveness of yourself and others. From this point you will finally be free.

But your normal became your warden. Your routine has imprisoned you and tied your hands and your feet, your creativity and your talent. It's time for you to forgive yourself and move on. In the words of **Shannon L. Alder:**

"You have to let go of what could have been, how you should have acted and what you wish you would have said differently. You have to accept that you can't change the past experiences, opinions of others at that moment in time. When you finally recognize that truth then you will understand the true meaning of forgiveness of yourself and others. From this point you will finally be free."

The greatest battle of life is the battle for your mind. The battle of the mind is for your focus. For the most part, people fail because of broken focus!

The Second Obstacle Is Distraction.

The greatest battle of life is the battle for your mind. The battle of the mind is for your focus. For the most part, people fail because of broken focus! Staying focused can help you accomplish your tasks, and help you resist the impulse to give in to distractions. Focus is power. A focused mind is difficult to stop from doing exactly what it sets out to do. Throughout his life, Joseph remained focused. He kept his eyes on the prize; the dream.

One of the things the enemy does not want us to do is to stay focused. He will do what he must do to create distractions.

Distraction is what prevents a person from giving his or her full attention to something; it is something that directs one's attention away from something else. It's an interruption to our concentration. It's shifting our attention from something of great importance to something of lesser importance. Distraction is the destruction of your dream in slow motion.

All of us have the tendency to be distracted. Even in the Scriptures, there's a long list of persons who experienced distractions of some sort:

- Eve was purposely distracted by the serpent with the forbidden fruit.
- Eve distracted Adam.
- Wine distracted Noah.
- Hagar and Ishmael distracted Abraham.
- Sodom distracted Lot.
- Looking back at the past distracted Lot's wife.
- Anger distracted Moses.

- Rebellious children distracted Eli.
- Women distracted Samson.
- Jezebel distracted Elijah.
- David distracted King Saul.
- Wealth distracted the rich young ruler.

We're becoming conditioned to distraction, and it's harming our ability to listen and think carefully, to be still, to pray, and to meditate.

Ever since the fall of man, people have had trouble staying focused, but today we live in an age of unprecedented distractions. We live in a busy world that puts in front of us endless distractions, including distractions from our faith. We're becoming conditioned to distraction, and it's harming our ability to listen and think carefully, to be still, to pray, and to meditate. This means that distraction is really becoming a spiritual danger. When we become distracted from our faith, we move further and further away from God.

Don't get caught up in the world's messy way of living. God is our source. God supplies what we need. Focus on Him, and when we do, it will allow Him to focus on us! Here's how He puts it in Matthew:

> *So don't worry about these things, saying, "What will we eat? What will we drink? What will we wear?" These things dominate the thoughts of unbelievers, but your heavenly Father already knows all your needs. Seek the Kingdom of God above all else, and live righteously, and he will give you everything you need.*

We serve God, and He serves us. We are His sons, and we are in covenant with Him. But when you live your life primarily for the enjoyment and pleasure it provides, you remove yourself further and further away from the Source. Instead, you choose to operate in the system of this world. Money is not a bad thing, but when your sole purpose in life is to attain it, then you become distracted from what God has called you to do. Don't let money, and the pleasures of this life, distract you from your dream!

The Third Obstacle Is Sexual Immorality.

> *And it came to pass after these things that his master's wife cast longing eyes on Joseph, and she*

> *said, "Lie with me." But he refused and said to his master's wife, "Look, my master does not know what is with me in the house, and he has committed all that he has to my hand. There is no one greater in this house than I, nor has he kept back anything from me but you, because you are his wife. How then can I do this great wickedness, and sin against God?" So it was, as she spoke to Joseph day by day, that he did not heed her, to lie with her or to be with her.*
>
> —GENESIS 39:7–10

Observe how she went from the eyes to the mouth. When she realized that the "eye ministry" was not effective, she resorted to the ministry of the tongue; she *spoke* to him day by day and he did not heed her, to lie with her or to be with her.

Many dreams die in the bedroom. Many men have lost their authority in the bedroom. Samson lost his strength, and it wasn't even in the bedroom; it was in a woman's lap. So, watch where you rest your head. Watch where you allow yourself to fall asleep. Do not compromise your dream for a few minutes of pleasure. Preachers are falling, politicians are falling, CEOs are falling all because of a few minutes of pleasure. Prostitution is big business now. It's big business because people who can pay big money are now in the business as clients. It's big business. If you have money, it is easy to find a prostitute. *Prostitution* by its very definition means a person who trades sex for money, which means that not all prostitutes are on the streets. People are prostituting themselves today for their rent money and their other monthly payments, and they are letting their dreams go. So sad!

One minute of pleasure for the wrong reason is not worth it. If that door closes because you said no God will open another door.

People can want you without wanting a future with you.

Jesus came to earth as God in the form of a man. He performed mighty exploits while here on the earth. He healed the sick, cast out demons, and raised the dead. However, in John 10:39, when the Pharisees tried to seize Jesus, He fled. It was not the time for Him to be captured. Jesus knew when to run. If you are going to survive the turbulent **in-between,** then you will also need to know when to run.

People can want you without wanting a future with you. People can be drawn to the favor on your life and be attracted to what your gifts, talents, and dreams can produce for their benefit. And they will do whatever it takes to profit off of what God has given you. You can't just give yourself over to somebody because they talk a good talk. You can't be that desperate for somebody that you trade your entire future to accelerate the progress of your dreams. God is still in control; He knows what you need. He knows what you can handle. He knows how well you have been equipped to master a situation. Don't you let anyone deceive you; be prepared to run!

Note verse 11: *But it happened, about this time, when Joseph went into the house, to do his work and none of the men of the house were inside,* ***she caught him by his garment.*** *"Come here boy, come lay with me, but he left his garment in her hands and fled and ran outside."*

He didn't get overwhelmed because the boss's wife wanted him!

We are talking about how to handle your **in-between.** Some stuff will show up in your life on your way to your dream, and if you don't know when to run, you could miss out on the fulfillment of your destiny. If you stay there, it will be a problem, so run.

Joseph ran outside and left his garment behind. Sometimes you may have to run and leave behind, something that you treasure. **A garment can't be more important than your dream.** Sometimes you may have to run and leave your heritage behind. Don't lose your dream while trying to protect your heritage. That's like giving up your future to protect your past. There may come a time when you may have to leave the job you love or give up the promotion you wanted in order to protect your dream. You may have to give up the increase in salary and run. You can't be that desperate for a few more dollars to the point that you are prepared to lose your dream for an increase in salary. That is professional prostitution. You've got to know when to run. God will take care of you!

People fall into all sorts of trouble chasing "true happiness." When true happiness is what God is offering, it's His joy and His peace wrapped up together. Happiness is when what you think, what you say and what you do are in harmony with each other. That means, then, that you **don't need a person to make you happy**, you don't need **a job or a title** to make you happy, and you don't need **money** to make you happy. So often what you are able to obtain in life is dependent on what you are able to walk away from. I left my heritage and I left a promised position simply to become a pastor in another denomination, and fifteen years later, I became second-in-command of an organization that is larger than the one I walked away from. You have to know when to run.

You can stay in a friendship or a relationship too long. When the season is gone, and you try to extend it, You will be putting yourself in the "danger zone."

You may have to run away from relationships, too. Relationships can be detrimental to you. They can be dream killers. The most dangerous thing you could ever want to be in your life is "**out of season.**" You can stay in a friendship or a relationship too long. When the season is gone, and you try to extend it, you will be putting yourself in the "danger zone." Seasons come, and seasons go. You have to know when seasons are gone. So, if you're not sure whether you should stay in a relationship or not, then simply ask God for wisdom. He'll tell you what you need to do in order for it to go the best way possible. It may still be hard but if someone is detrimental to you and your dream, then you have to let them go. Knowing when to run will save you and your dream. Think of it as a strategic withdrawal. It's far wiser to avoid temptation than to prove your mastery over it. You're able to focus your faith, attention, and efforts on accomplishing your dream instead of resisting temptation. This is why it is found in the Lord's Prayer: *"In this manner, therefore, pray:*

> *Our Father in heaven, hallowed be Your name. Your kingdom come. Your will be done on earth as it is in heaven. Give us this day our daily bread. And forgive us our debts, as we forgive our debtors.* ***And do not lead us into temptation,*** *but deliver us from the evil one. For Yours is the kingdom and the power and the glory forever. Amen"* (MATTHEW 6:9–13 NKJV).

Even Jesus knew it was smarter to avoid the temptation than to go looking for it. So, if you find yourself in the middle of a temptation…run!

The Fourth Obstacle Is Discouragement.

Any time you are close to accomplishing something or any time you are at the place where something is about to break, you will, more than likely, find yourself in the valley of discouragement.

Discouragement comes most often when you do the right thing, but experience poor results.

Discouragement comes when you work hard, but you make little or no progress.

Discouragement comes when you show up to practice every day, giving it your all, but you still lose the game.

Discouragement comes when you spend time studying and preparing for the exam, making major personal sacrifices, and you still fail.

Discouragement has the potential to eat a hole in your heart...to make you want to quit.

Discouragement is still one of the devil's greatest weapons.

Disappointments will come and go, but discouragement has a tendency of lingering around until you break it.

Here's what Dr. Charles Stanley had to say about discouragement:

> "Nobody can make you discouraged; it is a choice that you alone make when facing disappointments."

Napoleon Hill once said, "What we hardly see, what most of us never suspect, is the silent but irresistible power which comes to the rescue of those who fight on in the face of discouragement."

Discouragement doesn't have to stop you. If you run into a wall, don't turn around and give up. Find a way to climb over it, go through it, or walk around it.

Discouragement and her sister, disappointment, are both normal emotions we all experience...even as anointed people.

Job felt discouraged with his wife and friends.

Elijah became discouraged with life's circumstances.

Jeremiah felt angry and discouraged with God when he believed God was against him.

Peter felt discouraged with himself when he realized that he wasn't as courageous as he thought he was.

Discouragement and disappointment are normal emotions we all experience.

Stephen Spielberg was rejected from film school 3 times. I'm sure he was discouraged but he had a dream and kept going and become one of the greatest film makers of our time.

Critics told **Beyoncé** she couldn't sing. She was so discouraged that she went through a state of depression. She kept dreaming, she kept on singing and she kept going. Today she is one of the most prolific singer and song writer in the music industry.

When your life looks nothing like your hopes and dreams, it can be so easy to become discouraged.

Ronald Reagan ran in the Republican Primaries several times before winning the Republican nomination. I'm sure, in the process, he was discouraged, but at age 69, he became President of the United States of America. He went on to win an additional 4-year term at the age of 73.

Oprah Winfrey had a rough and often abusive childhood. As a young adult, **she was fired from a job as a television reporter because, according to her boss, she was "unfit for TV."** Of course she was discouraged, but she kept on dreaming and today, OPRAH is known as one of the most iconic faces on television as well as **one of the richest and most successful women in the world.**

Walt Disney had a rough start. As a teenager, he was **fired by a news paper editor because, according to him,**

he had no imagination and no good ideas. He was discouraged, but he kept dreaming and went on to create Walt Disney World which today rakes in billions every year from merchandise, movies and theme parks.

When a people are discouraged, they feel less confident, less hopeful, and less inclined to keep moving. When your life looks nothing like your hopes and dreams, it can be so easy to become discouraged. We have to remember that the God who gave us the dream is the God who is big enough to see that dream through to its completion in our lives. The Bible says as much:

> *Being confident of this very thing, that He who has begun a good work in you will complete it until the day of Jesus Christ.*
>
> —PHILIPPIANS 1:6 (NKJV)

We all experience issues in our lives, and these issues, if we are not careful, can cause us to become discouraged. Often, when we get discouraged, it is because we are focusing on the wrong things.

The lives of Joseph, David, Daniel, and many others show that life is an interesting mixture of good and bad. There will always be circumstances that are out of your control. Things will happen to you that you had nothing to do with. There are times when you will have to stand up for what you believe in, even if it costs you your job, your influence, or even your life. However, there are times when standing up like that is not a good choice. Sometimes the best option you have is to run.

CHAPTER 9

Prosper Where You Are

The journey from dreaming to a fulfilled dream can be long and filled with obstacles. We have discussed people, circumstances, and pleasures that can be hindrances to fulfilling your dream. But, it is also so important to learn how to make the most of where you are. Friends, you must do everything you can to come to the place in your life where you stop wasting your time complaining about where you are. Stop crying, weeping and mourning over what your circumstances are. Let the truth be told: **each of us has at least one challenge in life.** There is nobody in this world who is issue-free. Nobody!

There are single women wishing they had a husband and married women who are trying to get rid of their husbands. There are some people wishing they had a job; there are others who want to change their jobs, and there are some who are wishing to get rid of their job. There are some who wish they were on vacation; there are some who regret they ever went on vacation because they didn't like what happened when they were gone. The grass always seems greener on the other side, and if you focus so much on your issues, you can think you're the only one who has them. The truth is, everybody has an issue; some people are trying to pay for their house, while others are trying to find a house. Some are trying to catch up on their mortgage, while others are trying to find a way of getting a mortgage. Some people are now trying to figure out how they are going to pay their tuition; other people are trying to figure out how they are going to pay the light bill.

Everybody has issues, everybody. It's all relative. You can spend your time crying over what has happened to you, question why this happened to you, cry over why "they" don't like you or why "they" aren't treating you right. If you choose to do so, you'll end up like the children of Israel, who spent forty long years complaining in the desert, never reaching the fulfillment of their dreams. They could have been thankful for the cloud by day and the pillar of fire by night. They could have been thankful for the manna they received daily, just enough shade not to perish, just enough heat not to freeze to death, just enough food to last them each day, and just enough water so they didn't die of thirst. Their **in-between** sounds a lot like ours, doesn't it? You may be living from paycheck to paycheck, but I would recommend taking a different approach than the children of Israel did. It didn't work out for them. Instead you must learn to prosper where you are.

I admonish you to fight off the desire to stand still, be unproductive, or be discouraged when faced with challenging circumstances. Learn to prosper where you are.

Joseph had to do this on many occasions:

> *So it was, when his master heard the words that his wife spoke to him saying, your servant did to me after this manner, that his anger was aroused. Then Joseph's master took him, and put him into the prison, a place where the king's prisoners were confined. He was there in the prison, but the Lord was with Joseph, and showed him mercy, and gave him favor in the sight of the keeper of the prison. The keeper of the prison committed to Joseph's hand all the prisoners who were in the prison. Whatever they did there it was his doing. The keeper of the prison did not look into anything that was under Joseph's authority, because the Lord was with him, and whatever he did, the Lord made it to prosper.*
>
> —Genesis 39:19-23 NKJV

Joseph was now in prison based on a lie, but the Lord made him prosper, even in prison. After surviving being sold by his brothers as a slave, living in a foreign country, and being expected to function as a slave, many would say that he had earned the right to be upset about being falsely accused. For many, this would have been the last straw. However, we can learn a lot from Joseph's response. **He maintained a good attitude and he prospered right where he was. You must prosper where you are until you get to where you belong.**

God has a plan and you shouldn't allow a pit, a prison, or a premature celebration of your failure to move you away from God's plan and away from your dream.

Now, a lot of people find it extremely challenging to make full use of adversity. They are on their way to their dream. They are close to the dream, and then an attack comes along and they go off course. They have been working their dream for years; they can see the light now at the end of the tunnel. They are within striking distance of fulfillment, and here comes an attack and they drop out. People do not accept the fact that wherever they are, they could prosper right there. You have to get to the place where you are not prepared to take shortcuts. You shouldn't drop your standards in order to shorten the process. God has a plan and you shouldn't allow a pit, a prison, or a premature celebration of your failure to move you away from God's plan and away from your dream. You cannot let your present state confuse you.

Joseph was in prison and he was prospering. You cannot let people imprison your spirit, your personality, your gift, or your anointing. You have to come to the place now where you cannot give up your personality, your assignment, your gifts, or your anointing because there are people around you who don't like you or who don't help you. When I was growing up, there was a popular statement that was frequently made: "Sticks and stones may break my bones, but words can never harm me." I'm not sure if that's true. If you live long enough, you will see that incorrect words can be dangerous. There are many people right now who have abandoned their dreams because of what other people spoke into them. The Word of the Lord says that the words that come out of your mouth are spirit and life; they can kill, and they can cure. You should not abandon your dream, lay down your personality, or stop being who you are just because somebody told you something negative or doesn't like what you represent. You shouldn't do that. To abandon who you are in order to be accepted by somebody else is like slapping God in the face and telling God that He didn't do a good job when He created you. Joseph remained consistent in every phase of his life, and even in punishment he found favor.

We have to not only be settled, but we also have to be convinced and satisfied that not everybody is going to support us, no matter how good and noble the cause is and no matter what our dream is. People have a right to determine whether or not they believe in us and in our dreams, but the fulfillment of our dreams, or better yet, the pursuit of our dreams should not be determined by who believes in us. We must go after our dreams even if we are going alone; even if we are the only ones to believe in them; even if we alone are convinced that these dreams came from God.

Nobody has the responsibility to fix and work out your life, except for God. And God does that through you. Even if for some reason you are locked up in prison, don't let your spirit go to prison. Don't allow your personality to go to prison, and don't allow your gift to go to prison. The prison I'm talking about is not a physical one. This prison is for your hopes and dreams; it is a cage constructed for you by your enemy. It may be constructed through your work, through your family, or through your friends. An example of such a prison could be a place where you feel you have been pushed literally to the back of the line for a promotion or in an office on the job or shunned in society because your resources are limited, and you are frustrated with what is happening. But you can work with what is in your hand. Remember when God asked Moses what was in his hand? What are you good at? Use your gift to the honor and glory of God!

Think about it. You may have the gift to sell your company's products better than others, but you have been pushed to the back because of jealousy. You may have a skill for encouraging persons to attend functions or meetings. You may have the ability to point people in the right direction to get results. You may be known for your gentleness and genuine kindness, or you may have the gift of becoming a true confidant. You may have administrative skills, skilled at the interpretation of dreams, a listening ear, a natural voice that soothes persons during a dilemma, or the ability to make money. You may be empathetic, have hidden wisdom on certain matters; you may even be a dreamer, or have the skill to push the company's vision forward. Notwithstanding, your supervisors may have presented your ideas as their own and have had you sidelined for fear that the executives may see your capabilities and wish to use you instead. In spite of how you have been treated, use your gift around persons you find yourself with. Prosper where you are and trust God in the process. God will vindicate you, one day! He has your back.

The second part of Proverbs 18:16 says:

*A man's **gift**...brings him before great men (NKJV).*

This means that your dream is the gateway to your favor, and while pursuing your dream, you could be in prison and prospering. You could be in the "**poorest**" season of your life, in the middle of a recession, and you can still find prosperity in your broke season.

One of the keys to prospering where you are, and maintaining a good attitude, is patience.

God is looking for people whom He can bless in a major way. You have to know how to make the best out of where you are. If God gives you an assignment, work at it until you get to your next assignment. In the midst of the process, your friends may leave you and your family members may desert you, but work where you are and prosper right there. If the odds are against you, turn the odds around and make them work for you. Make your obstacles respect you. The odds are supposed to be against you—that's why they are odds. Joseph didn't have any money in his pocket, but God made him prosper. A word from God and favor in your life are more important than money in your pocket.

One of the keys to prospering where you are, and maintaining a good attitude, is patience. If you have a dream that has inspired you and a faith that you know can sustain you, then I want to assure you that you serve a God who will never leave you. Dreams are conceived long before they are ever achieved. You hardly achieve a dream overnight. Let me remind you that Joseph had his dream in chapter 37. Immediately after the dream, he was confronted with envy and hatred; he faced a conspiracy to be killed. He was thrown into a pit, and he was sold into slavery by his brothers, all because he had a dream. Your dream is bound to cause you some trouble before you ever see its fulfillment, but it is going to take patience to get there. Anything worth achieving will automatically have pain and disappointment attached to it. Some people will definitely disappoint you and cause you pain while you are on your way to your dream because usually, before you get to the fulfillment of your dream, you will go through a season when you witness the complete opposite of what you have been dreaming. It's the **in-between.**

Not only good things happen in our lives. As a matter of fact, most major inventions were created in pain and out of disappointment. Sometimes people have to be forced out of a job for them to recognize they have hidden talent. Sometimes a person's back has to get right up against the wall for them to know they are skilled at drawing holes in walls. If you don't push a bird out of its nest, it will never fly. That's why, like I mentioned in an earlier chapter, you cannot view destiny only from the perspective of all the good things that happen in your life, but you have to also include the negative things and know that God has the power to make them all work together for your good. You must be patient and trust God to see you through, to work it all out for you in the end.

You have to be patient when it comes to your promotion. After Joseph was thrown in prison, the warden put him in charge of all of the prisoners who were underneath him. And this type of promotion is where a lot of people, especially believers, lose the *real* promotion because they don't understand what is going on. You know the Scriptures say that promotion comes from God. When God is getting ready to promote you, He sometimes gives you a lesser promotion first, but if you don't show appreciation for the lesser promotion, you rarely get the real one that you're looking for. This was not what Joseph desired. He didn't want to be in charge of anyone in the prison. As a matter of fact, he didn't want to be in prison at all. But, he was in the prison, and he was promoted in the prison.

Friends, we have to learn how to recognize a promotion when it does not come with pay. God oftentimes gives signs. God hardly ever does anything for believers haphazardly; He gives us signs, He gives us warnings, and He gives us signals. Joseph was in prison being promoted and prospering, and he wasn't upset because he was still in the prison. Your promotion may only be a sliver of what you have been believing God for, but it's not time to be discouraged and think, "So this is it?" Instead you need to say, "The same God who brought me this promotion will bring me the fulfillment of the dream—that bigger promotion! The God who brought me this increase is the same God who will give me the greater increase." This should encourage your faith, but the enemy would seek to use this blessing of God to discourage you instead of encourage you. How wicked! So, don't be fooled; instead praise God for every inch of ground you are able to gain in faith.

The ultimate example of patience we are presented with throughout the Bible is that of ***"sowing and reaping."*** When we talk sowing and reaping, sometimes we only think about money. Joseph sowed his time and gifts to interpret the butler's and the baker's dreams, and he eventually made his way into the palace. Let me implore you to sow your time, gifts, or finances during your **in-between;** God will reward you. During your **in-between,** if you are in an office setting and are not where you want to be, remove yourself from negative thoughts and actions and work unto God. Go beyond the call of duty. Be kind to one another in spite of your circumstances. You do not know who is watching.

God's Word says in Galatians 6:7 (NKJV):

> *Do not be deceived, God is not mocked; for whatever a man sows, that he will also reap.*

It might be difficult, but sow good seeds, and God will give you strength. You will reap a positive outcome. The most powerful seed you can sow is what we will talk about in our next chapter, *service.*

CHAPTER 10

Serve Your Way into Fulfillment

Now, up to this point we have been with Joseph as he dreamed his dreams, was betrayed by his family, thrown in a pit, sold as a slave, promoted to the head of Potiphar's house, accused of sexual assault and thrown in prison. So, his reputation had been ruined and his freedom stripped from him. If this was where his story ended, it would have been a sad story, indeed. But, this wasn't the end of his story! Joseph went on to be promoted to being head of the prison underneath the warden. Subsequently, he met the prisoners, Pharaoh's baker and butler. Both of them had dreams that troubled them. God gave Joseph the interpretation of those dreams. They basically revealed to the baker that he was to be executed, and to the butler that he was to be reinstated to his prior position. After Joseph told the butler the interpretation of his dream, he asked the butler to keep him in mind when he got out.

After some time had passed, the Pharaoh had a dream that nobody could interpret. As a last resort, the butler finally remembered and told Pharaoh about Joseph. Joseph told the Pharaoh the meaning of his dream: that there would be seven years of plenty, and then seven years of famine. Because of his ability to interpret the Pharaoh's dream, Pharaoh promoted Joseph from being a prisoner to being second-in-command of all of Egypt. Joseph's new task, among others, was to oversee the saving of the food in the years of plenty, and the distribution of the food in the years of famine: a position that he used to bless his family and his people, a position that he used to make Egypt more prosperous than any of the surrounding nations! Even though that journey was long and treacherous, Joseph maintained a good attitude, avoided the obstacles thrown his way, remained faithful, kept his integrity and character intact, and ultimately trusted in God. He trusted in the dream God had given him, and he was able to see the realization of that dream! There was one constant action that Joseph performed in the beginning, throughout the duration of his **in-between,** and especially in the end, and that was service. With every level to which you are promoted, with each greater degree of authority you are given, with every ounce of responsibility that you are awarded, it's to the same level, degree, and amount of service you're able to give. We are not the ones who promote ourselves. Our hard work, determination, and abilities are not what land us higher positions in the kingdom of God. God is the One who promotes. It's our humility and our service to the Lord that cause us to accelerate toward our dream and increase in every area of our lives.

> *Humble yourselves therefore under the mighty hand of God, that he may exalt you in due time.*
>
> —1 Peter 5:6 (KJV)

> *And whatsoever ye do, do it heartily, as to the Lord, and not unto men; Knowing that of the Lord ye shall receive the reward of the inheritance: for ye serve the Lord Christ.*
>
> —Colossians 3:23–24 (KJV)

Humility and service go hand in hand.

Humility and service go hand in hand. Whether you are flipping hamburgers or preaching up on a stage, you should be working as unto the Lord! Whether you see any ministry value in it, your hard work, good work ethic, integrity, and character that you display in the workplace honors God. And if your boss at work never sees it, your real Boss in heaven does. Humility is so important here because it qualifies you for promotion in the eyes of God. Humility doesn't mean treating yourself as unimportant or spending time talking about how low and inadequate you are. Humility takes reality into account; your abilities, talents, gifts, mind, body, and even your very existence were given to you by God. So, how can you take credit for what is done through your life? You give glory to God because that's who deserves all the credit! When people look to you for leadership and you are constantly pointing them to God, then, as God increases your position, increases your funds, and increases your influence, He is gaining access to all of that here on this earth. When you gain money, God gains money, because you are His good and faithful servant.

Serving unlocks the doors to your future.

Joseph learned these valuable lessons at every stage of his journey. Joseph did not throw away his time while he was in his **in-between.** Instead, he made it a point to serve people, and work unto the Lord every step of the way. True leadership is being a servant and leading other people to their most successful, peaceful, and joyful places. True leadership has nothing to do with us and everything to do with the people we are leading and/or serving. This is not something that should cause us to be downtrodden! It's something we should be excited about and operating in all the time. Joseph served his father and even his brothers in the beginning; he served his way up through the ranks of being a slave, doing more than enough for Potiphar's house. Then he served in the prison, eventually being put in charge over the prison, second only to the warden, and he served the prisoners there by checking in on why they were discouraged and by interpreting their dreams. He served Pharaoh, giving Pharaoh the interpretation of his dream; then he served Egypt by organizing the food supply for the next fourteen years. He was able to serve his family and God's people. His whole life was filled with service, but if Joseph had not served faithfully when he was a slave, he never would have been put in charge of Potiphar's affairs. And after he was thrown into prison, no doubt the warden knew about Joseph's talents, and the Bible even tells us that the warden could see that God was with

Joseph. If he had not been serving faithfully at Potiphar's place, he wouldn't have been able to be put in charge of the prison. If he hadn't served faithfully at the prison, he never would have met and interpreted the dreams of the butler. If he hadn't served faithfully by interpreting Pharaoh's dream, the leader of a land who had done nothing but harm to him… then he never would have been promoted to second-in-command. If he hadn't served faithfully while second-in-command, he never would have been able to serve his family and God's people. Serving unlocks the doors to your future. Joseph wasn't living to get ahead in life; he was living to help others get ahead. His family bowing down to him did not puff him up with pride, and his dream did not elevate him in his own mind. Instead, he realized the responsibility it meant to care for his family.

The best way to get to your destiny is to place yourself in the service of others.

Story after story in the Bible puts a premium on honor and on service, not because those in authority over you on this earth are worth it, but because they serve the Lord, and their work is unto God, and their service and diligence will bring honor to God.

Even as David was anointed king, the journey to the throne required him to serve the present king, King Saul. The best way to get to your destiny is to place yourself in the service of others. The sooner we come to the understanding that we have been put on this earth to be a blessing to other people, the better off we'll be and the more fulfilled we will become. Serving others brings fulfillment.

In our world today, and even in the Church, there is an insatiable appetite for leadership, to be in charge or to be served. Sadly, this way of thinking is diametrically opposed to what we are called to be and do. Jesus was a perfect example of being a true servant. The Scriptures state:

> *Who, being in the form of God, thought it not robbery to be equal with God: But made himself of no reputation,* ***and took upon him the form of a servant****, and was made in the likeness of men:*
>
> —Philippians 2:6–7 (KJV)

Jesus came from heaven, down to earth, not to rule, but to serve. It is a sad thing to live your entire life like it's all about you. It would be wise to take a page out of the book of the Master Teacher, JESUS. He gave Himself. He died so that we might live. He became poor, the Bible says, so that we might become rich. He gave up His Kingly crown; He stepped down from His throne; He came down to a sinful, ungrateful, and unfriendly world, simply to redeem mankind. He paid a debt He did not owe, because we owed a debt we could not pay. That's the life of Jesus; He spent His life **giving** and **serving.**

When He saw blind people, He gave them sight;

When He saw deaf people, He gave them hearing;

When He saw dumb people, He loosened their tongues;

When He saw lame people, He made them walk;

When He saw hungry people, He performed miracles and fed them.

He spent His entire life **giving** and **serving.** When it became time for Him to die,

He gave His back to the cross;

He gave His head to the thorns;

He gave His hands to the nails, and

He gave His spirit to His father.

He spent His whole life giving, serving, and living for others.

The best way to find yourself and achieve your destiny is to see yourself in the service of others.

According to Gordon B. Hinckle, "One of the great ironies of life is this: The person who serves almost always benefits more than he or she who is served."

Friends, I have come to understand that one of the greatest joys of living is allowing your life to cause other people to rise higher and live a better life for themselves. That is why I love what the Lord has called me to do. I get the privilege of being under God's anointing when I preach. I see people being transformed and broken people being mended. I get to see people who came from a bad experience picking up the pieces of their lives and getting back on their feet. I've seen people who have been wounded from bad relationships, and a year or two later, I see them walking to the altar with somebody else, telling them I'll love you for the rest of your life. This all happens by the power of the Word of God! God allows me to be a part of His supernatural power being manifested here on the earth. While I love what I've been called to do, this is not where serving started for me. I served in Sunday school as a teenage teacher. I served in the youth department as a youth leader. I served as a choir director and musician at a time when remuneration was not even a consideration. I served as an assistant Pastor. I served as a personal ade to my father in ministry, and for twenty years, I served my Presiding Bishop. Nothing was too menial for me to do for either of them.

As a former business executive, as a presently serving Sr. Pastor, as a sitting Presiding Bishop, God has certainly been good to me. God has entrusted me with much. I truly believe, it had much to do with my **serving.** You have to serve your way. Here's what Dr. Martin Luther King Jr. had to say, **"Everybody can be great because anybody can serve. You don't have to have a college degree to serve. You don't have to make your subject and verb agree to serve. You only need a heart full of grace. A soul generated by love." He connected greatness with serving. That's a powerful concept.**

According to Gordon B. Hinckle, "One of the great ironies of life is this: The person who serves almost always benefits more than he or she who is served."

I love what I have been called to do because preaching is hardly ever about the preacher; **it's about the transforming, saving power of the Gospel of Jesus Christ,** or at least it should be. Paul said, in **Romans 1:16:** *"For I* *am not ashamed of the gospel, because it is the power of God that brings salvation to everyone who believes.*"

Whenever you are in a position where you receive favor, you must serve diligently and with a good spirit. If somebody gives you favor, don't live your life to the point that the person who gave you the favor comes to regret it.

Allow me to point you to this passage from Genesis 39 yet again.

> **1** And Joseph was brought down to Egypt; and Potiphar, an officer of Pharaoh, captain of the guard, an Egyptian, bought him of the hands of the Ishmeelites, which had brought him down thither.
>
> **2** And the LORD was with Joseph, and he was a prosperous man; and he was in the house of his master the Egyptian.
>
> **3** And his master saw that the LORD *was* with him, and that the LORD made all that he did to prosper in his hand.
>
> **4 And Joseph found grace in his sight, and he served him:** and he made him overseer over his house, and all *that* he had he put into his hand.

Here was Joseph in Potiphar's house as a slave with an amazing attitude. Potiphar, **the owner of the house,**

found favor with him. Joseph's response to the owner's favor, was to serve him. Look at what Potiphar did as a result of Joseph's service. **The Bible says that he made him overseer of the house, over all that he had he put under his command.** Everybody else in the house was under Joseph's command. **He was a slave with authority.**

Never underestimate the power that is in you and your ability to impact the world.

Everybody wants a title. They want somebody to call them by their title. My name is Neil Clarence Ellis, and even if you call me a something that's demeaning, I will still be Neil Clarence Ellis with or without my title. Who you are is not in your title; your title is your identification of what you do. Who you are **comes from what's in your spirit.** When I die, I hope more people know Neil Ellis than those who know Bishop Neil Ellis. When people know you by your title, they will treat you according to your job description. More often than not, you are more than your title proclaims. So many people have come to despise others based on their title. So often a person's title identifies them only by what they are doing while they are on their way to their destiny. They need something to pay their bills and to maintain their integrity on the way to the fulfillment of their dream. You can't rate them by their title or their job description, **because only God knows where they are headed.**

Never underestimate the power that is in you and your ability to impact the world. Never underestimate what it is you have to offer the world. Never underestimate YOU. You are greater than what you give yourself credit for.

God is uniquely forming a life assignment within you. This means that your existence is becoming a living message to others.

All the things that have made up your life:

- The various circumstances,
- The nagging problems,
- The defeats and victories,
- Those things that have made you proud,
- Those things that have humbled you,
- Those things that have made you weep,
- Those things that have exhilarated you.
- These elements are the building blocks that God uses to shape your life assignment.

My friend, I want to liberate you. Watch your attitude. Whatever you do, be a servant. Be a doctor-servant; be a banking-servant; be a lawyer-servant; be a preacher-servant; be a *servant* because if you can't serve, chances are you will never arrive. You've got to **serve** your way into your fulfillment. You can't just sit back saying, "I have this dream, and I am waiting for its fulfillment. God showed me a dream. He told me I was going to do this." But you are sitting back waiting for everybody else around you to come to your aid.

When God gives you an assignment, you can't look at what other people are doing, and get frustrated over what God has given to you. You must serve your way into fulfillment! I wish every young preacher of the gospel would take note of this, because young preachers today want instantaneous success. They want to be an overnight wonder. It does not happen like that. Take a look at the life of Jesus. Luke 3:23 states that Jesus was "about **thirty** years of age" at the start of His ministry. Take a look at everything He did before then. He worked, served, observed the ills of society, blessed people in various ways, and learned at the feet of His elders, but He also humbly shared His views with the scholars/teachers of that day and talked diligently with His Father. You have to serve other preachers and serve the people of God; you've got to serve your church and serve your way into fulfillment. So many people want to be served, and serving others is nowhere on their mind. But, you have to learn how to serve your way into fulfillment; in whatever company you currently work for! I want to remind you of these words found in Genesis 39:5:

> *So it was from the time that he had made him overseer of the house, and all that he had, that the **Lord blessed the Egyptians' house for Joseph's sake.***

Leaders, shareholders, and owners of companies are supposed to be grateful that there is a Christian on the staff. Instead, what's happening is the Christians are stealing just like the non-Christian employees. The Christians lie to get sick days when they are really traveling, just like the non-Christian employees. The Christians violate their lunch hours. The Christians react negatively to discipline or correction just like non-Christian employees. So, owners and supervisors are putting everybody in the same category. Some pastors can't even get their own church members, who are full-time staff members, to work diligently in the church ministry that they are a part of and being paid to do. This should not be!

When was the last time you worked longer than scheduled without asking for remuneration? When was the last time you voluntarily went in an hour early without anticipation of recognition or remuneration?

When was the last time you adjusted your own personal schedule to complete your assignment? If you already have a servant's heart... then you are well on your way!

God wants to bless whatever you are in charge of, whether it is personal or professional! For many of you, the fulfillment of your dream is going to place you in charge of something, but God will give you practice on your way to fulfillment. By the time you walk into your destiny and fulfill your dream, you are going to be the owner of something. **God is not going to let you wait until you get to the place of fulfillment, to own something or to be in charge of something substantial.**

For your diligence we see the following in Proverbs 13:4: "*The soul of the sluggard craves and gets nothing, while the soul of the* ***diligent*** *is richly supplied.*"

We are admonished in Galatians 6:9: "*And let us not grow weary of doing good, for in due season we will reap, if we* **do** *not give up.*"

Now, there is something to be said regarding how you handle your promotion. Let's look at Genesis 39:1–3 to see how Joseph handled his: "*Now Joseph had been taken down to Egypt, and Potiphar an officer of Pharaoh, captain of the Guard, an Egyptian bought him from the Ishmaelites who had taken him down there. The Lord was with Joseph, and he was a successful man, and he was in the house of his master, the Egyptian, and his master saw that the Lord was with him, and that the Lord made all that he did to prosper in his hands."*

Now note verse 4: *"So Joseph found favor in the sight of the master, and served him, then he made him overseer of the house, and all that he had, he put under his authority."*

Alright, look at Joseph now in this text and what he has. He has favor. With whom does he have favor? He has favor with the owner of the house. Look at how he handled the favor. He served his master. Now, that is not a common twenty-first-century pattern of behavior. We flaunt it, and oftentimes, we abuse it. We have to let the world know that we have the boss's private cell number, and oh, look at what I got for my birthday or Christmas. Some can't wait to let you know they have "carte blanche" with the boss. Because we have favor, we report to work late; because we have favor, we go home early; because we have favor, we take chances... like when the boss is out of town and we do not show up to work, or we come in and let everyone see you and then disappear.

As I reflect on the story, I realize that Joseph was a trustworthy young man. We can take a page out of this part of his life's story. You realize that he had the opportunity to be dishonest, but he did not take it. Now, you know in today's society there are few that exist like him in all sectors of life. He had total access to his master's wealth; everything, except his master's wife. You really have to manage FAVOR!

Favor made Joseph serve. He was appointed overseer of the entire operation, because his attitude, his perspective, and his work ethic were in the right place. He had favor, and when he got favor, **he did not lose** what caused him to gain the favor. He had served faithfully before the favor, and he kept on serving faithfully after the favor.

It's time to serve your way into your destiny.

CHAPTER 11

It's Time to Dream Again!

Now that you have heard how to deal with your **in-betweens,** it's time for you to dream again. Don't think I am unaware that we all have experienced feelings of hopelessness and despair. Like Joseph, you may feel as if you are in a pit where others have thrown you and squashed any hope that you had for achieving your dream. The only words you hear are filled with negativity, with others conspiring either to kill or to sell off your dream. Perhaps you can't help but identify with Joseph when he was a slave—where you own nothing and you work to survive from paycheck to paycheck. You may have felt that no matter what you have done in your life, trying to get ahead, making solid business, personal, and character decisions, every time you take a step forward, it seems like life knocks you three steps back. Joseph surely had to fend off the same thoughts and feelings. You may feel as if you had your dream for a moment, that you were doing what you loved and you had finally gotten to a place where you no longer had to worry about grocery money, paying the rent, and stressing about your finances. But then, like Joseph, you go from being the head of your boss's business to the jail cell, worse off than you ever were in the first place. Whatever stage of Joseph's life that you can identify with the most, whatever area that you find yourself in that is causing you to struggle and causing you to want to give up and give in, that's causing you to want to let go of your dream. Don't let it take hold of you!

The world as we know it has been shaped by dreams. All the great achievements of the world were once considered to be impossible.

See, that's what Satan is after. He knows he can't defeat you directly. He knows of the dangers that a man or woman with a dream can cause. He knows what the journey to accomplish your dream will work in you and through you. And he's afraid! Fear is all he knows, and if you'll let him, he will work it in you, too.

He's afraid of your faith being challenged and of your becoming victorious.

He's afraid of your heart being awakened to the intimacy of a close relationship with your Father.

He's scared of your passion igniting your creativity on how best to help the lives of those around you.

He's afraid of your character and integrity being refined in the midst of trying times.

He's afraid of your dreams becoming a reality and you fulfilling your destiny.

He's afraid of you influencing your generation, reshaping your nation, and ultimately bringing honor to God.

He knows he can't stop you, so he wants to nullify your effectiveness then steal your dream. He's a thief, and his number-one strategy is to surround your five senses with contradictions to what it is God has said to you.

He seeks to separate you from your faith, from your hope, and from your love through your circumstances. He knows he doesn't stand a chance against God's covenant partners, so, instead, he tries to get you to give up on your dreams. He wants to convince you that what you see is truer than what God has said. He wants it to be a "fact" that it's simply just not possible for you to accomplish your dream. The world as we know it has been shaped by dreams. All the great achievements of the world were once considered to be impossible. A man with a dream is a lot more powerful than a man with the facts. Facts said that electric lights were impossible, but Edison's dreams made them a reality. Facts said that man would never fly, but the Wright Brothers' dreams changed all of that. So, whatever your personal dreams are, don't let something as trivial as facts stand in your way. Remember the words of Jesus:

> *Jesus glanced around at them and said, With men it is impossible, but not with God;* ***for all things are possible with God.***
>
> —Mark 10:27 (AMP)

You have everything it takes right now to accomplish your dream.

So, don't give in to the lies of your enemy. You may be in the pit, a slave, or in jail. You may feel like the world is against you, and that there are thousands of miles between you and your dream. You may have given up on your dream, and now you think it's too late. But I'm here to tell you that while you have breath in your lungs, it's never too late. If you are alive, then there is hope for you, and there is hope for your dream. It matters not to what degree you have yielded to the feelings of fear and discouragement, or how badly you have messed up, or how impossible it may seem for your dreams to be fulfilled, God is bigger than all of it, and nothing in existence can separate you from His love for you. He is always on your side, and He is always ready to help you achieve your dream. It's never too late to pick up your dream; your passions are still there. Like I mentioned earlier in the book, God's gifts and His callings can never be rescinded. You have everything it takes right now to accomplish your dream.

Like Joseph, you may have been knocked down several times, but with each step that he got knocked back, he was really taking one step closer to his destiny. With every discouragement Satan threw his way, every test and trial that he experienced, Joseph chose to view it as opportunities to bring honor to God with his choices, his attitude, and with his faith. The best part is, you do not have to start over at square one. With all the faith that you have applied to that dream in the past, with all the time you spent talking about it, stirring up your passion and studying about it, none of that is wasted or for no purpose. Every effort you have put forth, and every effort you will put forth in God's name, is accredited to you! Read it for yourself:

> *Therefore, my beloved brethren, be firm (steadfast), immovable, always abounding in the work of the Lord, always being superior, excelling, doing more than enough in the service of the Lord, knowing and being continually aware that your labor in the Lord is not futile. It is never wasted or to no purpose.*
>
> —1 Corinthians 15:58 (AMP)

Let your dream be so big that it would require the power of God to accomplish.

Many people have had dreams that have died, dreams that have been buried under hurt, pain, and disappointment. They feel like such a failure, they think their life is over and that they will never rise again. But, it's time to dream again! It is time to forget the past, the hurt, the rejection, the business failure, the pain and it is time to start dreaming again. **There is no law in heaven or on earth against dreaming more than once. Don't just dream again, but this time, let your dream be big enough for God to get involved with it. Let your dream be so big that it would *require* the power of God to accomplish.**

In what areas of your life do you really need to be believing God? For what have you been believing God? It's time to dream again!

Too often we stop dreaming because we convince ourselves, It's not possible. We imagine more than we dare to dream or ask for. We put a limit on ourselves and therefore we impose a limit on God, too.

So, let me set the record straight:

- YOU have more strength than YOU believe.
- There is more fight within YOU than YOU know.
- YOU have far more potential than YOU could ever dream possible.

You have WITHIN YOU, the strength, the faith, the courage, and the power to dream a dream that has never been dreamed before.

You have **WITHIN YOU**, the **strength**, the **faith**, the **courage, and the power to dream a dream that has never been dreamed before. It is our time to dream again!**

If God is truly able to do exceedingly and abundantly above all that we can ask or think and He is, then whatever your dreams are, they will never be so great that God cannot meet them or exceed them. The fact that "exceeding" is in front of the word "abundant" implies that "abundant" is not even a word big enough in meaning to describe what God is able to do.

But look at how He does it:

Now to Him who is able to do exceedingly abundantly above all that we ask or think, according to the power that works in us...God is able to do!

That should be enough to have our hearts beat with confidence and faith! Our God is able to do more than what we can ask or imagine. Our God is able to do abundantly more than all we ask or imagine. Our God is able to do FAR MORE ABUNDANTLY BEYOND ALL THAT WE COULD EVER THINK!

It's time to face your **in-between** head-on. It's time to embrace the gap between where you are and where you're going and to start chipping away at that distance. Start living the fulfilled life that God has called you to live and start enjoying your journey! Regardless of what lies your enemy and this world have tried to convince you are true, please allow me to set the record straight. You have more strength in you than you believe; there is more fight within you than you know; and you have far more potential then you could ever imagine is possible!

Listen to the dying words of D.L. Moody to his sons: ***"If God be your partner, then make your plans big."***

There is a spirit of faith behind that quote! Your next chapter in life is just waiting to be written. There are so many questions just waiting to be asked. There is a whole new lifestyle just waiting to be embraced. And there is a new depth of God just waiting for us to discover.

CHAPTER 12

Created to Solve a Problem

God has given to each of us a life assignment! Each of us has been called to something. Each of us has a distinct mission to fulfill while we are here on this earth, and God has perfectly equipped each of us to realize that life assignment. Every one of us has a specific purpose for coming into this world, and within that specific and personalized purpose lies our destiny.

You are more than who people have been saying you are, and you are greater than what you've been giving yourself credit for.

You have not been shortchanged. You have everything you need to fulfill your assignment. Never underestimate the power that is in you and the ability that you have been given to impact this generation.

Never underestimate the worth and value of what it is you have to offer this world. Never underestimate YOU. You are more than who people have been saying you are, and you are greater than what you've been giving yourself credit for. The truth is, you are carrying inside of you an assignment that will impact three to four generations after your life—believe me!

WHO ARE YOU?

Ephesians 2:10 says:

> "For we are His workmanship, created in Christ Jesus for good works, which God prepared beforehand that we should walk in them."

1. You are God's workmanship, His masterpiece, His prized possession.
2. You were created in Christ Jesus.

3. You were created for good works.
4. You were created to walk in them.

God did all of these things for you before you were conceived. You are not a mistake! You are not just another person! You are not your job description!

You are not what people have said you are! You are God's masterpiece, God's prized possession.

Jeremiah 1:4–5 says:

"Then the word of the LORD came unto me, saying,
Before I formed thee in the belly I knew thee; (and before thou came forth out of the womb I sanctified thee, and I ordained thee a prophet unto the nations.)"

And Psalm 139:13–16 says:

"For You formed my inward parts; You covered me in my mother's womb.
I will praise You, for I am fearfully and wonderfully made;
Marvelous are Your works, and that my soul knows very well.

> *My frame was not hidden from You, when I was made in secret, and skillfully wrought in the lowest parts of the earth,*
>
> *Your eyes saw my substance, being yet unformed."*

Let us consider the premium that God has placed on your life. God said: "Before I formed you in the womb, I knew you; My eyes saw your substance, being yet unformed…and at the appropriate time, I formed you…fashioned you…and shaped you… I protected you…brought you safely out of your mother's womb. And at every phase of your development, I've had my eyes on you. When you were born, I breathed into your nostrils the breath of life…and when I did that, I placed within you everything you will ever need to fulfill your life's assignment."

Because you existed in God before the foundation of the world; because you were given your assignment while you were still in the mind of God; because your life assignment is so significantly necessary, God assigned you before He created you. Because God Almighty spoke to you about the plans He has for you before you were born, don't assume for one minute that God did all of that for you just to be another number. Ohhhh no! Because you are who you are, there is nothing going on in heaven right now without YOU in mind. Nothing!

The truth is though, the enemy of God wants to break you down. He wants to break your ability to dream. He wants to destroy the creative power that's in you before you get the revelation that it's there. It doesn't matter to him whether you are a Christian or not, he is working overtime to make sure that your life depresses you; your marriage depresses you; your single status depresses you; your divorce depresses you; and/or your children depress you. But, as you prepare to pursue your dream, God is reviving, restoring, refreshing, and refilling you for your **in-between.**

The world is waiting for you to write that book, start that business, release that CD or DVD, complete that computer program, or launch that global online business.

Life is a series of problem-solving opportunities.

Remember, Psalm 139:13 says:

"For You formed my inward parts; You covered me in my mother's womb."

The psalmist says that God formed you. That word "formed" denotes that He took great care and gave special attention to creating you. It paints the picture of a potter expertly crafting his art at the potter's wheel.

Please note that everything God forms, He fills.

He formed the universe and filled it with planets.

He formed the seas and filled it with fish.

He formed the sky and filled it with stars and clouds. He formed man and filled him with breath and organs. Whatever He forms, He fills.

He formed you and filled you with talents, gifts, ideas, and strategies. You are gifted, talented, and full of ideas and strategies. In other words, when God formed you, He filled you with solutions.

Life is a series of problem-solving opportunities. However, there is no problem that you will ever face that you are not anointed to solve. So often, God allows situations to come into your life in order to DIRECT you, CORRECT you, PROTECT you, and PERFECT you.

You have been gifted, anointed, and blessed in order to make someone else's life better.

Everything God created is a solution to a problem. Your eyes see. Your ears hear. Your nostrils smell. Doctors solve physical problems. Mechanics solve car problems. Dentists solve teeth problems. Lawyers solve legal problems. Mothers solve emotional problems.

You were created and anointed to solve a problem for someone, somewhere, at some point in time. You have been gifted, anointed, and blessed in order to make someone else's life better. Translation: You were created to solve a problem.

The life of Joseph was one of great problems and trials.

- His brothers conspired against him.
- He was thrown into a pit.
- He was sold as a slave.
- He was falsely accused of rape.
- He was thrown into prison.
- He was forsaken by his family, forgotten by his friends, and frustrated by his failures.

Why did these things happen to a young man who was guilty of nothing more than doing the will of God? All of the things that happened to Joseph were a part of God's plan for his life. Joseph was anointed to solve a major problem. All that happened to him was designed to get him to the place where he could solve that problem.

All of your pain, problems, and persecution have been positioning you for this period of promotion.

For the most part, that's what's been happening to you. All of your pain, problems, and persecution have been positioning you for this period of promotion.

In Genesis 41, the spirit of Pharaoh was troubled because of the dreams he was having. He called for the magicians of Egypt and all its wise men. But, no one could interpret the dreams for him. Meanwhile, Joseph was in prison and had no idea of what was happening in the palace. However, what was happening in the palace was what was going to get him out of the prison. He had absolutely no idea that within twenty-four hours, he would get a divine hookup and a major breakthrough.

Please know that even as you read this book, God is sovereignly working behind the scene on your behalf.

The fact that you don't see it happening; the fact that you don't know anything about it; the fact that you don't know what's next; the fact that you don't know what in the world God's doing, doesn't mean that there's nothing happening. God is at work in your life, sovereignly working behind the scene on your behalf.

In Genesis 41:9–14, Pharaoh's chief butler talked to him about an experience he had with Joseph while in prison. He advised how Joseph interpreted his dream and the baker's dream and everything turned out just like he said.

In verses 15–16, Joseph was summoned to appear before Pharaoh.

In verses 17–24, Pharaoh told Joseph his dreams.

In verses 25–32, Joseph interpreted Pharaoh's dreams.

In verses 33–37, Joseph gave Pharaoh some advice.

Pharaoh took the advice, and look at his response:

> *"Then Pharaoh said to Joseph, 'Inasmuch as God has shown you all this, there is no one as discerning and wise as you.*
>
> *"'You shall be over my house, and all my people shall be ruled according to your word; only in regard to the throne will I be greater than you.'*

> *"And Pharaoh said to Joseph, 'See, I have set you over all the land of Egypt.'*
>
> *"Then Pharaoh took his signet ring off his hand and put it on Joseph's hand; and he clothed him in garments of fine linen and put a gold chain around his neck.*
>
> *"And he made him to ride in the second chariot which he had; and they cried before him, Bow the knee: and he made him ruler over all the land of Egypt."*
>
> —GENESIS 41:39–43

Overnight, the season for Joseph changed. Overnight, there was a supernatural turnaround in his circumstances. Overnight, Joseph had gone from a place of obscurity to a place of authority. Overnight, Joseph went from the prison to a place of prominence. Overnight, he went from being a prisoner to become the prime minister.

God sent him there for something bigger than his signet ring, his hold chain, his private chariot, his powerful office, his bank account, or his own notoriety. Although these were all benefits of his new office, they were not the primary purpose for him being placed in that role. His assignment was bigger than that. He was put in place to solve a problem. This problem was centered around the famine in the land that had also hit Canaan. At that time, there was only one place in the region that had food for sale, and that was Egypt. Joseph was in charge of sales and distribution. His brothers, on the instructions of their father, went to Egypt to buy food, and they all ended up in front of Joseph.

Observe Joseph's conversation with his brothers, as recorded in Genesis 45.5–7:

> *"'Now therefore be not grieved, nor angry with yourselves that you sold me here for God sent me to preserve life.*
>
> *"'For these two years the famine has been in the land, and there are still five years in which there will be neither plowing nor harvesting.*
>
> *"'And God sent me before you to preserve a posterity for you in the earth, and to save your lives by a great deliverance.'"*

There are two things over which you have complete dominion, authority, and control: your mind and your mouth.

Joseph was put where he was to solve a major problem. You were also created to be a problem solver. If you don't like how things are in your life, change them. If you're sick and tired of being sick and tired, you are a problem solver, so solve the problem! If you're tired of weapons being formed against you and tongues rising up against you, remember that you have the power to condemn them and move on. The weapons of our warfare are not carnal but mighty through God to the pulling down of strongholds. As a problem solver, you have the power to pull them down! But the greatest power you have is in your mouth. Life and death are in the power of the tongue.

As a problem solver, you have the power to speak those things that are not as though they are. There are two things over which you have complete dominion, authority, and control: your mind and your mouth. If you decree a thing, it shall be established for your sake (Job 22:28).

In biblical times, particularly in the Old Testament, it was the king who had the authority to make decrees. A decree was a written document that was very specific and clear about the subject matter. It was law, and it had to be carried out according to the king's wishes. That means that the person making the decree had to be in a position of power and authority to carry it out.

This Old Testament principle of decreeing (in writing) is not commonly practiced today by the New Testament believer. The New Testament believer is more accustomed to the practicing the principle of declaring as opposed to decreeing.

To declare means to make known one's position or to announce officially or to state emphatically. For the most part, the New Testament believer is of the view that we have been authorized, in the name of Jesus, to declare a thing and to expect that what has been declared will be carried out. That means we say that it will be established, manifested, revealed, or shown to be true as was declared by the Christian believer.

Why don't you take a moment now to release some things into the atmosphere? As for me, I declare:

> "I'm on my way to my destiny!"
>
> "God is going to finish what He started in my life!"
>
> "God is taking me to a place where I've never been before!"
>
> "I'm getting ready for life on a whole new level."
>
> "I have been equipped to handle my **in-between.**"

ABOUT THE AUTHOR

Bishop Neil C. Ellis is the presiding prelate of the Global United Fellowship (GUF), with more than 1,400 churches in 42 countries. GUF serves as an international body of spiritual leaders, fellowships, and congregations united to strategically plan, implement, and execute transformative and generational change.

Bishop Ellis is the senior pastor of Mount Tabor Church in Nassau, Bahamas. This church has grown from 11 charter members in 1987 to thousands of members and thousands more who are a part of the Internet Church, Mount Tabor Anytime. As a pastor to pastors, he mentors a large number of pastors around The Bahamas, Europe, and the United States and serves as a counselor and advisor to hundreds of pastors around the world.

Bishop Ellis has been recognized by Her Majesty, Queen Elizabeth of England for rendering distinguished services in Commonwealth nations and is also the recipient of the 2010 Trumpet Award for Spiritual Enlightenment. He is the youngest living inductee in the International Civil Rights Walk of Fame located in Atlanta, Georgia. He is also the author of several books and is a much sought after conference speaker and prophetic teacher.

Bishop Ellis and his wife reside in Nassau, Bahamas along with their two children.

Neil C. Ellis Ministries
Pinewood Gardens & Mt. Tabor Drive
P O Box N-9705
Nassau, Bahamas

Email: info@neilellisministries.com

Local Tel: 242-392-9305/6

International Tel: 954-703-4828